MASTER YOUR MEMORY

BOOKS, VIDEOS AND AUDIO CASSETTES
BY TONY BUZAN

Books
Use Your Head
Speed Reading
Make the Most of Your Mind
The Evolving Brain with Terence Dixon
Use Your Memory
The Brain User's Guide
Spore One (poetry)

Videos
Use Your Head
The Enchanted Loom (the Evolving Brain)
Soweto 2000

Audio Cassettes
Learning and Memory: Psychology Today
S.E.A.L. Conference 1987

MASTER YOUR MEMORY

Tony Buzan

David & Charles
Newton Abbot   London   North Pomfret (Vt)

Dedicated to my dear friends in the Brain Clubs and
Buzan Centres

With especial thanks to Vanda North for her dedication to and support of the concept,
and for playing the memory games with me; to Lorraine Gill, the Artist, for her
brilliant research and constant inspiration; to my Personal Assistant Carol Coaker and
Research Assistant, Phyllida Wilson, who literally wrote much of this work, and to
my Editor, Tracey May, for a memorable performance!

British Cataloguing in Publication Data

Buzan, Tony
  Master your memory.
  1. Mnemonics
  I. Title
  153.1′4   BF385

  ISBN 0-7153-8974-2
  ISBN 0-7153-9034-1 (paperback)

Phototypeset by Typesetters (Birmingham) Ltd
Smethwick, West Midlands
and printed in Great Britain
by Billings & Sons Ltd, Worcester
for David & Charles Publishers plc
Brunel House Newton Abbot Devon

Published in the United States of America
by David & Charles Inc
North Pomfret Vermont 05053 USA

CONTENTS

INTRODUCTION 6
1 THE BASIC PRINCIPLES OF MEMORY SYSTEMS
   (MNEMONICS) AND HOW THEY WORK 9
2 THE MAJOR SYSTEM 19
3 THE SELF-ENHANCING MASTER MEMORY GRID (SEMMG) 22
4 ARTISTS 29
5 COMPOSERS 39
6 WRITERS 56
7 SHAKESPEARE 75
8 VOCABULARY 98
9 LANGUAGES 103
10 COUNTRIES/CAPITALS 129
11 KINGS AND QUEENS OF ENGLAND 133
12 ELEMENTS 134
13 RED WINES OF BORDEAUX 150
14 SOLAR SYSTEM 161
15 MEMORISING YOUR LIFE 165
   APPENDIX 174

INTRODUCTION

A student sat enthralled. It was the first lesson of his first day at University. In front of him the Professor was calling the roll:

'Abrahamson?'	'Here, sir!'
'Adams?'	'Here, sir!'
'Barlow?'	'Here, sir!'
'Bush?'	'Here, sir!'
'Buzan?'	'Here, sir!' . . .

There were two things different on this morning from the normal roll call in a class: first, the Professor was standing in front of his own desk, his hands clasped firmly behind his back, with no list of students' names in front of him; second, when he came to the next name, 'Cartland', and there was no response, he did *not* move on to 'Chapman', but paused for a moment his hands still clasped behind his back, his eyes looking straight at the students, and said *'Cartland*!? . . . Jeremy Cartland, address 2761 West Third Avenue; phone number 794 6231; date of birth September 25th 1941; mother's name Jean, father's name Gordon; . . . *Cartland*!? Absent!'

And so the Professor continued, calling the roll without hesitation, and wherever a student was absent, even though he had never seen them before, and could have had no way of knowing, on this first day, who was going to be present and who not, presenting the entire list of data about the absent student as he had done with Cartland. All the students knew that he knew, in the same astounding detail, the same basic biographical detail about each of them.

When he had completed the roll with 'Zygotski?' 'Here, sir!', he looked at the students with a wry smile and said

'That means Cartland, Chapman, Harkstone, Hughes, Luxmore, Mears, and Wilsby are absent . . . I'll make a note of that sometime!!'

And so saying, he turned and left the room in a stunned silence.

To the enthralled student it was one of those moments where a life's 'Impossible Dream' became possible: the dream of training his memory so that it could, in a multitude of special situations, function perfectly.

To be able to remember the names and dates of birth and death and all the important facts about the major artists, composers, writers and other 'greats'!

To be able to remember languages!

To be able to remember the giant catalogues of data from biology and chemistry!

To be able to remember like that Professor!

To be able to remember any list he wanted!

He hounded the Professor for two months until he was finally given the first basic lessons in what he was later to learn were the mnemonic techniques developed by the Greeks.

For the next 20 years he devoured everything he could on memory, creativity and the nature of the human brain, with the vision constantly in mind of a New Super System: a giant, enjoyable and easy to use, super-grid memory system that would act as a data base allowing everyone to have immediate access to whatever major information structures were important to them.

After 25 years, the New System Emerged.

The enthralled student was me.

The one to whom I offer it, with delight, is You.

The Approach

In order to start you on what will probably be one of the major intellectual and mental adventures of your life, the first section of the book has been structured to give you background information, and to lead you step by step to the Self-Enhancing Master Memory Grid.

First you will be shown how Memory (mnemonic) Systems started with the Ancient Greeks, and how they were developed to the current day.

Next you will be introduced to the Basic Memory Principles, which will give you the fundamental building blocks with which to structure your new super-power memory. This will be combined with a concomitant development of all your senses.

Following this you will be introduced to the most updated modern brain research, especially that involving the left and right hemispheres and the upper and lower brain. Here you will find how the Basic Memory Principles tie in closely with our modern knowledge of how your brain works.

Armed with the knowledge of how the principles work, of how your senses can be enhanced, and of how your brain skills can be used appropriately, you will be given examples of how to apply the principles. These will be developed into two basic systems, the Link System and the Peg Systems, which will enable you to practise what you have learnt on memorising the Planets of the Solar System, and basic lists of ten items.

From this you will be taken to the first significant Memory System – the Major System. It is this system that has been used by most of the world's top mnemonists and memory performers. The Major System allows you instantaneously to remember 100 items.

The step from 100 to 10,000 may seem like an impossible dream. To show you that it is *completely* possible, you will be guided through recent experiments to prove that your brain can remember not only 10,000 items but even more with incredible accuracy.

These experiments will be supplemented with information on some of the great brains in history, with examples of their memory feats. Their brains were the same as yours; they simply knew how to use them in the manner outlined in *Master Your Memory*.

By this stage you will be ready and capable of absorbing comfortably the Self-Enhancing Master Memory Grid. Having mastered the grid, you will then be able to attach to it all the significant lists of information you will ever wish to know, and in the very act of so doing you will not only be making your 'memory muscles' even stronger, you will also be increasing your powers of concentration and creativity.

We begin with the Basic Laws and Principles.

CHAPTER ONE

THE BASIC PRINCIPLES OF MEMORY SYSTEMS (MNEMONICS) AND HOW THEY WORK

The Background

Before modern brain science had revealed, neurophysiologically and psychologically the extraordinary power and potential of the human brain, the Greeks had discovered that by using certain techniques, mental performance could be enhanced enormously.

The Greeks developed fundamental memory systems called mnemonics, a name derived from their worship of the Goddess of Memory, Mnemosene.

These mnemonic techniques were exchanged between the intellectual elite of the time, and were used to perform prodigious feats of memory in public that gained the performers personal, economic, political and even military power.

The techniques were based on fundamental principles that were, while being both easy and enjoyable to apply, profound in their effect on memory improvement:

The Basic Mnemonic Principles

The Greeks discovered, by introspection, discussion, and exchange, that memory was in major part an ASSOCIATIVE process; that memory worked by linking things together. For example, that as soon as your brain registers the word 'apple' it remembers the colours, tastes, textures, and smells, etc, of that particular fruit.

The Greeks further discovered that these associations, these links, could be made stronger and more long lasting as long as certain basic principles were applied:

1 ASSOCIATION Whatever you wish to memorise, make sure you associate or link it to something stable in your mental environment.

2 IMAGINATION Einstein said, 'Imagination is more important than knowledge'. The more you apply your imagination to memory, the better your memory will be.

3 EXAGGERATION In all your images, exaggerate size, shape, and sound, etc.

4 CONTRACTION Where appropriate, make things microscopically small. The very uniqueness of the miniscule makes it more memorable.

5 HUMOUR The more funny, ridiculous, absurd and surreal you make your images, the more outstandingly memorable they will be.

6 MOVEMENT In any mnemonic image, movement adds another giant range of possibilities for your brain to 'link in' and thus remember.

7 SEXUALITY We all have a good memory in this area!

8 ORDER AND SEQUENCE In combination with the other principles, order and sequence allows for much more immediate reference, and increases the brain's possibilities for 'random access'.

9 NUMBER Numbering adds specificity and efficiency to the principle of order and sequence.

10 SUBSTITUTION Substituting a more meaningful image for a more normal or boring image increases the probability of recall.

11 SYNAESTHESIA Synaesthesia refers to the blending of the senses. Most of the great 'natural' memorisers, and all of the great mnemonists developed an increased sensitivity in each of their senses, and then blended these senses to produce enhanced recall. In developing the memory it was found to be *essential* to sensitise increasingly and train regularly your:

   a) Vision
   b) Hearing
   c) Sense of smell
   d) Taste
   e) Touch
   f) Kinaesthesia – your awareness of bodily position and movement in space
   g) Positivity

In most instances positive and pleasant images were found to be better for memory purposes, because they made the brain want to return to the images. Certain negative images, even though applying all the principles above, and though in and of themselves 'memorable' could be blocked by the brain because it found the prospect of returning to such images unpleasant.

Modern Confirmation of the Greeks
Recent brain research, especially in the area of the left and right cerebral hemispheres, has confirmed that each one of us has, distributed throughout the most evolutionarily advanced part of our brain, an enormous range of mental skills that simply require appropriate training and development for them to manifest and grow. These 'left and right brain skills' include the following:

1 Language
2 Order
3 Sequence
4 Number
5 Logic
6 Linearity
7 Analytical ability
8 Rhythm
9 Colour
10 Imagination
11 Re-creation
12 Dimension

In the lower and mid-brain, and distributed in part throughout the upper brain, exist our additional mental abilities to:

1 See
2 Hear
3 Smell
4 Taste
5 Feel
6 Move in dimensional space

11

A quick check confirms the extraordinary similarity between what the Greeks discovered by self-analysis and practice, and what modern science has discovered through the elegant rigours of the Scientific Method.

Armed with this double confirmation, it is possible to apply the Mnemonic Principles with greater confidence and greater efficiency, guaranteeing improvements in your memory and general mental performance that once were considered the stuff only of an unobtainable Utopia.

Putting the Mnemonic Principles to Work

In attempting new memory tasks, it is advisable to apply the mnemonic techniques to areas where people have been regularly presented with certain information, have regularly attempted to memorise this, and have regularly failed.

One such area concerns the Planets of the Solar System.

In the last five years I have researched this memory area extensively, and have found that in an audience of a thousand people, the following statistics apply:

1 900 people out of 1,000 have learnt and at some time memorised the Planets.
2 In each individual's lifetime, they have been 'exposed' to this information, either in school, or through the various forms of media, for a total number of hours ranging between 10 and 100.
3 100 out of 1,000 *think* they know how many Planets there are in the Solar System.
4 40 out of 100 know they know how many.
5 20 *think* they know the order of the Planets from the Sun to the farthest Planet.
6 10 out of 1,000 would be willing to bet on it!

The reason for this staggering loss of knowledge lies in the fact that most of the Mnemonic Principles were not applied when the information was first given.

Check your own knowledge and experience in this particular memory task:

Did you learn the Planets of the Solar System, and if so, how many times and over what period of time?

Do you know the currently accepted number of Planets in the Solar System?

Do you know the normal order of the Planets in the Solar System?

Memorising the Planets of the Solar System
Now that you have learnt the basic memory principles from both the Greeks and modern brain research, you are going to apply them, and thus practise and prepare yourself for using the Self-Enhancing Master Memory Grid to the Planets of the Solar System.

There are nine Planets.

In order from the Sun, they are:

1 Mercury (small)
2 Venus (small)
3 Earth (small)
4 Mars (small)
5 Jupiter (big)
6 Saturn (big)
7 Uranus (big)
8 Neptune (big)
9 Pluto (small)

In order to memorise the Planets *for life*, you simply apply most of the Mnemonic Principles, creating in your imagination a linked and fantastic story. If you follow it carefully and completely, it will be harder for you to forget than to remember!

Imagine that over the space where you are currently reading, there is a giant thermometer, and that suddenly the glass containing the silver measuring liquid breaks and covers the floor and furniture around you with tiny (because the Planet is small) balls of that liquid metal: **MERCURY**.

Rushing in to see what has happened comes an incredibly beautiful, scantily clad, little (because the Planet is small) exquisitely perfumed goddess whose name is: **VENUS**.

Venus plays like a child with the scattered mercury, and finally manages to pick up one of the mercury globules. She is so delighted that she throws it in a giant arc, which you follow

13

JUPITER (5)

MARS (4)

EARTH (3)

VENUS (2)

MERCURY (1)

PLUTO (9)

NEPTUNE (8)

URANUS (7)

SATURN (6)

with your eyes, until it lands in your garden, which confirms that the third Planet is: **EARTH**.

Because of the power of her throw, and the height of the arc, when the globule lands it creates a small crater which sprays earth (EARTH) into your neighbour's garden.

Your neighbour, a little man (because the Planet is small) becomes unreasonably angry about the event, and charges out into the garden brilliantly red faced (because the Planet is red) astoundingly angry, and in a mood for total war. The God of War is your fourth Planet: **MARS**.

Just as Mars is about to attack you, you are saved. For striding on to the scene comes a giant so large and powerful that he shakes the very foundations (and you must *feel* them) of where you are. He tells Mars to calm down, which Mars immediately does, for this new giant is your friend as well as being the king of the Gods: the fifth big Planet **JUPITER**.

As you look up to the hundred foot high Jupiter, you see emblazoned in flashing gold letters across his enormous chest, the word SUN. Each of these gigantic letters stands for the next three big Planets of the Solar System: **SATURN, URANUS, NEPTUNE**.

Sitting on Jupiter's shoulder thinking the entire episode has been hilarious, is a little (little because the Planet is small) Walt Disney dog by the name of: **PLUTO**.

Re-run this fantasy in your mind, and then see how difficult it is to forget!

In the continuing studies of people's memorisation of the Planets, it was found that before memorising them with the Mnemonic System:

a) 800 out of 1,000 people didn't really care about the Planets and seldom paid attention to information about them.

b) 100 out of 1,000 felt vaguely to be very interested in the Planets.

c) 100 out of 1,000 were actively disinterested and/or disliked the Planets!

After memorising the Planets with the Mnemonic System, virtually 1,000 out of 1,000 became actively interested.

This on-going study illustrates the very significant fact that if the human brain receives data that is rapidly forgotten or becomes confused, it will reject further data in that subject area. As time progresses, the more and more information that is presented to the brain in the given area, the more it will block that information and will learn increasingly less, often eventually blocking the information altogether.

If the brain, on the other hand, has information in organised and memorable grids, each new bit of information will automatically link to the existing information, naturally building into patterns of recognition, understanding and memory that we call knowledge.

For example, if you hear that a space probe has been sent to Venus, and you do not know where Venus lies within the Solar System, the first thing your brain will be confronted with is confusion. You will not know which way the probe has gone from the Earth, whether Venus is hot or cold, what its relationship is to the Sun and why anyone should send a space probe there in the first place. As a consequence, you will react by basically rejecting the information.

If, on the other hand, you *know* that Venus is the second Planet out from the Sun, and is the one inside Earth's orbit that is nearest to Earth, you will know that as the space probe goes to Venus, it will be going to a Planet that is nearer to the Sun and therefore hotter than Earth. Your mind will therefore have a mental image of direction, temperature, and nearness to Earth, and will *automatically* make appropriate associations. At the same time as your mind is doing this, it will also be subconsciously, and in many cases consciously, reviewing and confirming your knowledge of the other Planets. Thus, the more you know, the more easy and automatically you begin to know more.

Thus it can be seen that in the second scenario, once a basic grid has been established, learning in the subject area continues to grow and expand throughout life.

Advanced Systems

The Mnemonic System for memorising the Planets is a basic Link System. The next stage of development after a Link System is a Peg System, which uses a special and permanent list of Key Memory Images, on to which you can attach whatever you wish to memorise.

One of the most basic of these is the Number-Shape System.

The Number-Shape System

In the Number-Shape System, you devise a Key Memory Image for each number, the images acting as permanent hooks for linkage. To create your system, you simply imagine a shape that is similar to or 'looks like' the number. For example:

1 = Paint brush
2 = Swan
3 = Two-humped camel
4 = Yacht
5 = Hook
6 = Elephant's trunk
7 = Flag
8 = Snowman
9 = Tennis racket
10 = Bat and ball

Let us say you wished to remember a simple shopping list, in which you wished to buy the following ten items:

1 Oranges
2 Bananas
3 Apples
4 Shoe polish
5 Toothpaste
6 A mug
7 Potatoes
8 Tomatoes
9 Flour
10 Bread

Using the Number-Shape System, and applying the Mnemonic Principles, you would memorise in the following way:

17

1 You might imagine a paint brush with which you are painting giant, house-sized oranges an even more brilliant orange, as you do so being swamped by the orange smell, and occasionally taking bites out of a giant orange, feeling and tasting the juices that run down your throat and chin.
2 Here you might imagine a swan flying with an incredibly large bunch of bananas in its beak, coming in to land on feet that become banana water skis.

The more you make these exaggerated images for yourself, the better, for personal association is virtually always more memorable than that suggested or given by someone else. With the remaining eight items, therefore, apply the Mnemonic Principles to the shopping list, making sure that whenever you are in doubt, you add more imagination and more sensuality. Once you have applied the memory principles to the memorisation of the list, check yourself, or get someone else to check you. Should you ever miss an item, go back to it, analyse where the weakness was, and strengthen your associations.

Increasingly Advanced Systems
From these basic Link and Peg Systems, the early practitioners of memory realised that far more advanced and sophisticated systems could be developed, and that the memorisation of much more complicated data could be made as easy as the memorisation of the Planets and a shopping list. One of the most successful of all such systems was the Major System, which is outlined in the next chapter.

CHAPTER TWO

THE MAJOR SYSTEM

The Major System was devised in the mid-seventeenth century by Stanislaus Mink von Wennsshein. Von Wennsshein's objective was to create a memory system that would convert numbers into letters and letters into numbers, thus allowing the memoriser to make words out of any combination of numbers, and numbers out of any combination of letters.

One of the major applications of this was devising a Peg System, similar to the Number-Shape System, but extending not only from one to 10, but from one to 100.

In the eighteenth century the system was modified and improved by an Englishman, Dr. Richard Grey.

In converting numbers to letters, the Major System has a special code, devised so that by its very nature it allows itself to be memorised! The code is as follows:

```
0 = 2, s, z, soft c
1 = d, t, th
2 = n
3 = m
4 = r
5 = l
6 = j, sh, soft ch, dg, soft g
7 = k, hard ch, hard c, hard g, ng, qu
8 = f, v
9 = b, p
```

The vowls a, e, i, o, u and the letters h, w and y do not have numbers associated with them and are used simply as 'blanks' or fillers in the Key Memory Image Words you will soon be creating.

The Major System's special code can be memorised by applying the Mnemonic Principles to themselves in the following way:

Memorising the Major System Code

---

0   The letter s, or z, is the first sound of the word zero; o is the last letter.

1   The letters d and t have one downstroke.

2   The letter n has two downstrokes.

3   The letter m has three downstrokes.

4   The letter r is the last letter in the word four.

5   The letter l can be thought of as either the Roman numeral for 50 or a hand with five spread fingers, the index finger and thumb forming an L shape.

6   The letter j is the mirror image of 6.

7   The letter k, when seen as a capital, contains two number 7s.

8   The letter f, when handwritten, has two loops, similar to the number 8.

9   The letters b and p are the mirror image of 9.

Once you have grasped the Special Code, it is possible to translate any number into any word.

For example, the number 43 translates to the letters r and m. Using one of the vowel 'fillers' (and in devising the system it is always best to try 'a' before 'e', 'e' before 'i', etc) you discover the word 'ram', which immediately translates back to the number 43.

Similarly, the number 82 translates to the letters 'f' and 'n'. Again using the vowel 'filler' you immediately have the word 'fan', which itself translates back to the number 82.

Using this approach it is easy to develop a system similar to the Number-Shape System, that allows you to generate 100 Key Memory Images, on to which you can then link whatever hundred items you wish to memorise.

The Major System One Hundred
Following is the Basic One Hundred.

It is important that you practise memorising them by referring in your Mind's Eye back to the Special Code, and that you have each word clearly *imaged* in your mind in order that it will be ready to latch on to any new information you wish to recall.

If you wish to substitute your own words for any words suggested, feel free to do so as long as your substitutions use the appropriate letters.

If you wish to draw little images, or make any key word notes around any of the Key Memory Words in the Basic 100, this will enhance your memory.

	s,z soft c	d,t th	n	m	r	l	sh,j,dg soft ch, g	k,hard ch,c,g	f,v, soft gh	b,p
	0	1	2	3	4	5	6	7	8	9
0–9	Zoo	Dew	Noah	Ma	Rah	Law	Jaw	Key	Fee	Pa
10–19	Daze	Dad	Dan	Dam	Dare	Dale	Dash	Deck	Dive	Dab
20–29	Nasa	Net	Nan	Name	Nar	Nail	Nash	Nag	Navy	Nab
30–39	Mace	Mat	Man	Ma'am	Mare	Mail	Mash	Mac	Mafia	Map
40–49	Race	Rat	Rain	Ram	Rare	Rail	Rash	Rack	Rafia	Rape
50–59	Lace	Lad	Lane	Lamb	Lair	Lily	Lash	Lake	Laugh	Lab
60–69	Chase	Chat	Chain	Chime	Char	Chill	Chacha	Check	Chaff	Chap
70–79	Case	Cat	Can	Cam	Car	Call	Cage	Cake	Cafe	Cab
80–89	Face	Fat	Fan	Fame	Fair	Fall	Fash	Fake	Fife	Fab
90–99	Base	Bat	Ban	Bam!	Bar	Ball	Bash	Back	Beef	Baby
100	Daisies									

From 100 to 10,000 in One Easy Bound!

Having established the Basic 100, it is now possible, using a system which helps memorise itself, to develop the 10,000 memory system: The Self-Enhancing Master Memory Grid (SEMMG).

On to this grid you will be able to attach any of your Master Lists. The following chapter explains how.

CHAPTER THREE

THE SELF-ENHANCING
MASTER MEMORY GRID (SEMMG)

Is It possible?

Before developing a system for the memorisation of 10,000 items, it is important to find out whether the brain can easily handle such a grid!

Both research and history indicates that the human brain can handle it with ease.

The Experiments

In 1970, Raif N. Haber reported the following experiment in *Scientific American*: subjects were shown a series of 2,560 photographic slides at a rate of one every ten seconds. The total of seven hours of viewing was split into several separate sessions over a period of days, and one hour after the last slide had been shown on the last day, the subjects were tested for recognition. They were shown 280 pairs of slides in which one member of each pair was a picture from the series they had seen, while the other was from a similar set which they had not seen. On average their recognition, even after such a drawn-out showing, was between 85 to 95 per cent accurate.

A second experiment was performed in which the presentation rate was speeded up ten times, to one image every second, and the results were identical!

A third experiment in which the new high rate of presentation was maintained, but the pictures were shown as a mirror image still produced identically high results.

Haber commented 'these experiments with pictorial stimulae suggest that *recognition of pictures is essentially perfect*. The results would probably have been the same if we had used 25,000 pictures instead of 2,500.'

In a further experiment reported by R. S. Nickerson in the *Canadian Journal of Psychology*, subjects were presented, at the rate of one per second, 600 pictures, and tested immediately after the presentation. Recognition accuracy was 98 per cent!

Nickerson expanded on this research, subsequently presenting subjects with 10,000 pictures, making sure that the pictures were vivid (i.e. applied the Mnemonic Principles). With the vivid pictures, subjects were recalling 9,996 out of a 10,000 correctly!! When these results were extrapolated, it was estimated by the experimenters that if the subjects had been shown a million pictures rather than 10,000, they would have recognised 986,300.

The conclusion was: 'the capacity of recognition memory for pictures is almost limitless, when measured under appropriate conditions', according to Lionel Standing in his article '*Learning 10,000 Pictures* in the Quarterly Journal of Experimental Psychology.

With this evidence, it becomes apparent that the Self-Enhancing Master Memory Grid, if used in conjunction with the Mnemonic Principles, can be handled by your brain with ease. Further evidence from the great memorisers confirms this viewpoint.

The Great Memorisers
The great memorisers had brains, it seemed, which were the same as everyone else's. They simply used them more effectively.

Antonio de Marco Magliabechi was able to read entire books, and memorise them without missing a single word or punctuation mark. He eventually memorised the entire library of the Grand Duke of Tuscany.

Professor A. C. Aitken, Professor of Mathematics at the University of Edinburgh, was able easily to remember the first thousand decimal places of the value of Pi – forward and backward.

The American, Daniel McCartney, in the nineteenth century, could tell, at the age of 54, what he had been doing on every day since early childhood. He could give the exact date, the weather conditions during the day, and tell what he had eaten for breakfast, lunch and supper on any given day.

Christian Friedrich Heinecken at the age of ten months was

able to speak and repeat every word said to him. By the age of three he had memorised most of world history and geography, and had similarly memorised Latin and French.

Paul Charles Morphy was a chess champion who could remember every move of every game that he had played throughout his championship career, including those he had played while blindfolded. His claims were backed up by the fact that nearly 400 of his games were preserved only because he was able to dictate them *long* after the event.

Themistocles was able to remember the 20,000 names of the citizens of Athens.

Xerxes was reputed to be able to recall the 100,000 names of the men in his armies.

Cardinal Mezzofanti, a nineteenth century linguist, was able to memorise the vocabulary of between 70 and 80 languages, including Latin, Greek, Arabic, Spanish, French, German, Swedish, Portuguese, English, Dutch, Danish, Russian, Polish, Bohemian, Serbian, Hungarian, Turkish, Irish, Welsh, Albanian, Sanskrit, Persian, Georgian, Armenian, Hebrew, Chinese, Coptic, Ethiopian, and Amharic.

The Shass Pollak Jews of Poland were able to remember the exact position on the page of every word in each of the twelve volumes of the Talmud.

Giant religious books such as the Talmud and the even larger Vedic scriptures of ancient India were also passed down by memory.

Knowing that both 'average' brains, when trained properly, and the Great Brains were and are capable of such apparently extraordinary feats, means that the SEMMG System is easily within your grasp.

The Self-Enhancing Master Memory Grid
The Self-Enhancing Master Memory Grid allows you, by using the very principles of Mnemonic Techniques themselves, to expand from 100 to 10,000 as quickly as you can visualise.

Using the Basic 100 from the Major System, you multiply this system by 10 and then by 10 again.

To do this you use both synaesthesia and basic knowledge grids as follows:

Thousands		0–99	100–199	200–299	300–399	400–499	500–599	600–699	700–799	800–899	900–999
0–99	**Vision**	0 –	1 Dinosaur	2 Nobility	3 Moonlight	4 Ravine	5 Lightning	6 Ocean	7 Concorde	8 Forest Fire	9 Paintings
1–199	**Sound**	10 Singing	11 Waterfall	12 Wind	13 Roar	14 Railway	15 Laughter	16 Chime	17 Car	18 Violin	19 Babbling Brook
2–299	**Smell**	20 Sea-Weed	21 Tar	22 Nutmeg	23 Mint	24 Rose	25 Leather	26 Washing	27 Garlic	28 Flowers	29 Pine
3–399	**Taste**	30 Spaghetti	31 Water	32 Wine	33 Mango	34 Rhubarb	35 Almond	36 Jam	37 Clove	38 Fish	39 Banana
4–499	**Touch**	40 Sand	41 Wetness	42 Honey	43 Mud	44 Rock	45 Oil	46 Jelly	47 Grass	48 Velvet	49 Bark
5–599	**Sensation**	50 Swimming	51 Dancing	52 Energetic	53 Melancholy	54 Warm	55 Loving	56 Shaking	57 Climbing	58 Flying	59 Happiness
6–699	**Animals**	60 Zebra	61 Dog	62 Newt	63 Moose	64 Rhinoceros	65 Elephant	66 Chimpanzee	67 Kangaroo	68 Fawn	69 Bear
7–799	**Birds**	70 Seagull	71 Duck	72 Nightingale	73 Magpie	74 Rooster	75 Lapwing	76 Chaffinch	77 Eagle	78 Flamingo	79 Peacock
8–899	**Rainbow**	80 Red	81 Orange	82 Yellow	83 Green	84 Blue	85 Indigo	86 Violet	87 Grey	88 Black	89 White
9–999	**Planets**	90 Sun	91 Mercury	92 Venus	93 Earth	94 Mars	95 Jupiter	96 Saturn	97 Uranus	98 Neptune	99 Pluto

0– 999	Vision	5000–5999	Sensation
1000–1999	Sound	6000–6999	Animals
2000–2999	Smell	7000–7999	Birds
3000–3999	Taste	8000–8999	The Rainbow
4000–4999	Touch	9000–9999	The Planets

For example, the zero to 999 you use **VISION** – in other words, you focus on your *seeing* the image you wish to remember as your key memory image. For 1000 to 1999 you use **SOUND**, focussing on your *hearing* for each image. For 2000 to 2999 you use your sense of **SMELL**, focussing in your memory images on this sense. And so on, for each thousand, using, subsequently, **TASTE, TOUCH, SENSATION, ANIMALS, BIRDS, THE COLOURS OF THE RAINBOW**, and **THE PLANETS**

For each separate 100 of each 1000, you have a specific Vision, a specific Sound, a specific Smell, etc. Thus, referring to the Grid on page 25, your specific visions for the separate 100s from 100 to 999 are Dinosaur, Nobility, Moonlight, Ravine, Lightning, Ocean, Concorde, Forest Fire, and Paintings.

For example, keeping 0–99 as your Basic 100 grid, and using nine Vision-images to get you from 100 to 999, you would do the following:

101 would simply be a giant dinosaur covered in dew; 140 would be a giant dinosaur in the middle of an incredibly noisy and thundering race. Whatever you wished to memorise as your 140th item would therefore be attached to this image.

Similarly, for 3000 to 3999, each separate hundred in the progression would have a Taste image attached to the basic hundred, in this instance Spaghetti, Water, Wine, Mango, Rhubarb, Almond, Jam, Clove, Fish, and Banana.

Moving up in the first 1,000, all still related to the first of your synaesthesia elements, Vision, all items from 700 to 799 would still be the basic code items, but in this instance connected to the image of Concorde. Thus 706 would be Concorde with its bent nose as a giant jaw; 795 would be Concorde with a giant ball for its wheels. Again, any image you wish to remember for 795 would be attached to this image.

Similarly each of the Sound, Smell, Taste, Touch and Sensation, etc, ten key words applies to the hundred items within its grid.

If, for example, you wanted to remember item 3650, your Key Memory Image would be a Lily covered with Jam, and you would imagine the Taste of that combination, and the image, connected to whatever you wished to remember.

When creating your images, which you should do as a game, as well as a mental exercise and mental brain training, make sure that in your key images for each of the different senses, you emphasise the sense. Thus, for 4,103, touch combined with wetness combined with ram, you obviously see the image of the wet ram, but your main memory device here is to *feel* the wetness of its fur, its horns, its muzzle, etc.

By using this Self-Enhancing Master Memory Grid, you will be not only developing a system that enables you to memorise 10,000 items with the ease of Haber and Nickerson's experimental subjects, but you will also be training each one of your sensory areas, which will have a profound and positive influence on all other aspects of your life.

You will be creating a positive spiral in which the more you practice your memory techniques, the more your general memory will improve; the more you add your knowledge lists to your memory grid, the more you will be increasing the probability of automatic learning; and the more you do all this, the more automatically *all* of your various intelligences and mental skills will be improved.

The following chapters outline many of the major memory lists which, like the Planets, are supposed to be learnt and usually forgotten. Once they are learnt, they form giant foundations from which your brain can, with the ease and facility of 'The Greats', continue on its journey to wisdom.

The chapters are as follows:

4 Artists
5 Composers
6 Writers
7 Shakespeare
8 Vocabulary

9 Languages
 10 Countries/capitals
 11 Kings and Queens of England
 12 Elements
 13 Red Wines
 14 Solar system
 15 Memorising your Life.

The suggested approach to the following Superlists, is to select the ones which you wish to memorise, organise your Self-Enhancing Master Memory Grid appropriately, and commence the exercise of remembering them. Throughout, apply the Mnemonic Principles.

From this point on, it is useful to keep a mental set open for any grids you might find that would be useful to you, and to make a habit of memorising at least one new list per year.

Should you wish to remember the grid itself, the Basic 100 can be used to memorise each of the key words in the grid, thus further using the system to memorise itself.

CHAPTER FOUR

ARTISTS

The great artists have spearheaded mankind's research into the nature of our perception. They have also recorded human history with an elegance at least equal to that of the literary historians. Knowing the names, birthplaces, dates of birth and death, and some of their famous works, places them, as you did with the Planets, in a context and perspective that allows you to automatically and continually learn more about them as you progress through life. Every time you see an advertisement for an art exhibition in future, the images and information pertaining to that exhibition and artists will add to your growing body of Art Knowledge, and will increase your knowledge of this most important area to your continuing advantage.

As Leonardo da Vinci said, if one wishes to develop an all round mind, make sure you do two things: 'study the Science of Art, and study the Art of Science'.

In memorising the great Artists, Composers, and Writers, you might, for example, choose SEMMG numbers from 1000 to 1300, if you had already used your first thousand, or if you wished to reserve the 1000 to 1999 grid especially for lists of famous great brains in the different disciplines. Let's assume that Leonardo da Vinci was your number 1020. Your SEMMG Key Memory Image is the number 20 (NASA) joined with the Sound-image of Singing.

To remember that da Vinci was a high Renaissance (rebirth) Inventor with one of his famous works being 'Virgin of the Rocks', you would image a rocket ship with da Vinci piloting it, *singing* an opera aria (to remind you that he was Italian), the rocket ship going particularly high, with a little baby by his side helping him at the controls. Your rocket would be going towards an imaginary planet to rescue a young virgin who was trapped in giant rocks. To remember the dates 1452 to 1519, you would take the numbers 4 = R, 5 = L, 2 = N; 5 = L, 1 = T or D, 9 = B, and make word images from them that related to da Vinci. For example, *R*enaissance *L*eading *N*aturalist; *L*eonardo *D*a Vinci's *B*urial.

Apply these principles and examples to memorising whichever of the major knowledge grids most appeals to you. From *Master Your Memory* it is recommended that you select at least six of the lists included, in order to get you off to a good start.

	Born	Died	Nationality
Giomo	1266	1337	Italian
Siena School			
Famous Works: Madonna & Child			
Enthroned with Angels (1285)			
Duccio, di Buoninsegna	1255	1318	Italian
Byzantine influence			
Martini, Simone	1284	1344	Italian
Siena School			
Linear Expressiveness			
Famous Works: Maesta (1315)			
Orcagna, Andrea	1308	1368	Italian
Florentine School			
Famous Works: Christ Rescuing the			
Disciples, Human Passion			
Ghiberti, Lorenzo	1378	1455	Italian
Florentine (Gothic) influence			
Famous Works: Baptistry Doors,			
Sacrifice of Isaac			
Donatello	1386	1466	Italian
Florentine Sculptor			
Famous Works: The David – Classical			
Influence			
Angelico, Fra	1387	1455	Italian
Florentine School			
Famous Works: The Descent from			
the Cross, Inspired Monk			
Uccello, Paolo	1396	1475	Italian
Florentine School			
Famous Works: The Battle of San			
Rumano, Perspective Geometry			
Weyden, Roger van der	1399	1464	Flemish
Netherlands			
Famous Works: The Descent from			
the Cross, Went to Rome on			
Pilgrimage			

	Born	Died	Nationality
Bellini, Jacopo	1400	1476	Venetian

Perspective
Famous Works: The Beheading of
John the Baptist, Pencil, Funded
Venetian Renaissance

	Born	Died	Nationality
Masaccio	1401	1428	Italian

Florentine
Trinity/Architectural
Perspective

Piero della Francesca	1410	1492	Italian

Mathematical Perspective
Famous Works: The Resurrection

Agostino, di Duccio	1418	1481	Italian

Sculptor
Famous Works: Tombs of Tempio
Maletestian in Rimini

Castagno, Andrea del	1419	1457	Italian

Florentine Perspective
Famous Works: Nine Famous Men
and Women

Bellini, Gentile	1429	1507	Italian

Venetian painter with father
and brother
Famous Works: Cycle of History
Pictures in Doge's Palace

Bellini, Giovanni	1430	1516	Italian

Venetian painter, very influential, best
of Madonna painters
Famous Works: Agony in the Garden

Antonello da Messina	1430	1479	Italian

Space extention
Famous Works: Sacra Conversazione

Botticelli, Sandro	1445	1501	Italian

Realistic
Famous Works: The Birth of Venus

Bosch, Hieronymus	1450	1516	Flemish

Fantasy
Famous Works: The Temptation of
St Anthony

Leonardo da Vinci	1452	1519	Italian

High Renaissance/Inventor
Famous Works: Virgin of the Rocks

Durer, Albrecht	1471	1582	German

Printmaker/Fine Detail & Perspective

31

	Born	*Died*	*Nationality*
Famous Works: St Jerome in his Study			
Bartolommeo della Porta, Fra	1474	1517	Italian
Became a Monk			
Famous Works: Last Judgement			
Michelangelo, Buonarroti	1475	1564	Italian
High Renaissance			
Sculptor/Painter			
Famous Works: Sistine Chapel, Lifelike work			
Giorgione	1476	1510	Italian
Modern Painting			
Famous Works: Laura in Vienna			
Raphael	1483	1520	Italian
Stylized/The School of Athens			
Andrea del Sarto	1486	1530	Italian
Painted light and shade			
Famous Works: Birth of the Virgin			
Titian, (Tiziano Vecelli)	1487	1576	Italian
High Renaissance			
Expressive painting			
Famous Works: Assumption of the Virgin			
Pontormo, Jacopo	1494	1556	Italian
Religious painter			
Famous Works: Deposition			
Holbein, Hans the Younger	1497	1543	German
Realistic/Influenced by Florence			
Famous Works: Dead Christ			
Tintoretto, Jacopo	1518	1594	Italian
Mannerist drawings			
Famous Works: Paradise			
Bruegel, Pieter	1525	1569	Belgian
Fantasy			
Greatest Northern European Artist of his time			
Famous Works: The Tower of Babel			
Barocci, Rederico	1535	1612	Italian
Counter-reformation			
Famous Works: Descent from the Cross			
El Greco, Domenikos Theotocopoulus	1541	1614	Greek
The Greek/Distorted expression			

	Born	Died	Nationality
Famous Works: Assumption of the Virgin			
Carracci, Ludovico	1555	1619	Bolognese
Founded Teaching Academy in Bologna			
Carracci, Agostino	1557	1602	Bolognese
Bolognese Engraver			
Famous Works: Last Communion of St Jerome			
Carracci, Annibale	1560	1609	Bolognese
Bolognese Painter			
Famous Works: Hercules at the Crossroads			
Caravaggio, Michelangelo Merisida	1571	1610	Italian
Naturalist			
Doubting Thomas/Painted Truth As He Saw It			
Jones, Inigo	1573	1652	
Architect			
Stage Scenery			
Rubens, Sir Peter Paul	1577	1640	Flemish
Allegory			
Self Portrait/Popular			
Famous commissions			
Hals, Frans	1581	1666	Dutch
Photographic/Pieter Van Den Broecke			
Psychological Insight			
Teniers, David	1582	1649	Flemish
Late Mannerist Painter			
Famous Works: Peter and St Mary Magdalen			
Poussin, Nicolas	1594	1665	French
Classical/Inspiration of the Poet/ Intellectual Painter			
Algardi, Alessandro	1595	1654	Bolognese
Bolognese sculptor			
Famous Works: Attila			
Zubaran, Francisco de	1598	1665	Spanish
Religious themes/Still life/Highly finished works			
Bernini, Gianiorenze	1598	1680	
Sculptor			
Theatrical Decoration/St Theresa/ Dramatic themes			

	Born	Died	Nationality
Velazquez, Diego Rodriquez de Silva	1599	1660	Spanish
Court Painter Philip IV			
Baltasar Carlos/Technical Brilliance			
Dyck, Sir Anthony van	1599	1641	Dutch
Court Painter Charles I/Charles I of			
England/Skilful Textures			
Claude, Gellée (Claude Lorraine)	1600	1682	French
Landscape/Flight into Egypt/Classical			
Dreams			
Champaigne, Phillipe de	1602	1674	Belgian
Brussels Portrait Painter			
Famous Works: Portrait of Daughter			
Brouwer, Adriaen	1605	1638	Flanders
Flanders, Painter of Sordid Tavern			
Scenes			
Rembrandt, van Pyn	1606	1669	Dutch
Portraitist/Self Portrait/Feeling for			
Humanity			
Murillo, Bartolome Esteban	1617	1682	Spanish
Religious paintings/The Two			
Trinities/Sentimental			
Lebrun, Charles	1619	1690	French
French Painter			
Famous paintings decorate			
Galerie des Glaces			
Vermeer, Jan	1632	1675	Dutch
Dispassionate Tranquility/Girl			
Reading/Perfect Pitch of Light			
Pellegrini, Giovanni Antonio	1675	1741	Venetian
Venetian decorative painter			
Famous ceiling for Bank of France			
Tiepolo, Giovanni Battista	1696	1770	Venetian
Allegory/Apothosis of the Prince			
Bishop			
Brilliant Draughtsman			
Hogarth, William	1697	1764	English
English Etcher/Painter/Satire			
Marriage A La Mode/Brilliant Social			
Comment			
Caneletto, (Giovanni) Antonio	1697	1768	Venetian
Urban Scenes-Venetian Life/			
Stonemason's Life/Recorded life in			
Venice			
Chardin, Jean Baptiste	1699	1779	French
Photographic/Breakfast Table			

	Born	Died	Nationality
Greatest 18th century Painter			
Latour, Maurice Quentinde	1704	1788	French
Pastellist			
Batoni, Pompeo	1708	1787	Italian
Neoclassic			
Famous Portrait: General Gordon			
Wilson, Richard	1713	1782	Welsh
Wales landscape painter			
Famous Works: Snowdon			
Reynolds, Sir Joshua	1723	1792	English
Portraitist/Nelly O'Brien			
First President of Newly			
Founded Royal Academy of England			
Stubbs, George	1724	1806	English
Animal Portraits/Lady and Gentleman			
in a Carriage			
Gainsborough, Thomas	1727	1788	English
Portraitist/Mr & Mrs Andrews/			
Grand Landscapes			
Mengs, Anton Raffael	1728	1779	Italian
Neoclassicism painter			
Famous Works: Parnassus			
Romney, George	1734	1802	English
Portrait Painter			
Famous Works: Lady Hamilton			
Barry, James	1741	1806	Irish
Historical paintings			
Famous Works: Progress of Human			
Culture			
Goya, Francisco de G y Lucientes	1746	1828	Spanish
Court Painter Charles IV			
The Maja Clothed/Painted Realities of			
War			
David, Jacques Louis	1748	1825	French
Neo Classical/Death of Marat/			
Political Subjects			
Flaxman, John	1755	1826	English
Neoclassic Sculptor			
Famous monuments Mansfield in			
Westminster Abbey			
Raeburn, Sir Henry	1756	1823	British
Portrait painter			
Famous Works: The Macnab			
Canova, Antonio	1757	1822	Venetian
Neoclassic Sculptor			

	Born	Died	Nationality

Famous Portrait: Pauline Bonaparte
Borghese as Venice

Blake, William — 1757 — 1827 — English
Poet/Artist/Visionary/God Creating
Adam/Broke with Renaissance
Tradition of Man as Centre of an
Ordered World

Lawrence, Sir Thomas — 1769 — 1830 — English
Portraitist/Queen Charlotte/
Brilliantly technical

Turner, Joseph Mallord William — 1775 — 1851 — English
Romantic Landscapes/Frosty
Morning/Atmospheric Painter

Constable, John — 1776 — 1837 — English
Suffolk scenes/Haywain/Paint the
Last of Pastoral England

Chantrey, Sir Frances — 1781 — 1841 — English
Sculptor
Famous Works: Bust of Walter
Scott

Gericault, Theodore — 1791 — 1824 — French
Romantic Art/Kraft of the Medusa/
Brief Life

Corot, Jean Baptiste Camille — 1796 — 1875 — French
Portraitist/Avignon/Impressions of
Italy and French

Delacroix, Eugene — 1798 — 1863 — French
Political Themes/Liberty on the
Barricades/Oriental Influences

Landseer, Sir Edwin — 1802 — 1873 — English
Sentimental painter of animals
Famous Works: Group of Lions at the
foot of Nelson's Monument, London

Courbet, Gustave — 1819 — 1877 — French
Painted political themes
Bonjour Monsieur Courbet/Part of
Anti Academic Movement

Bocklin, Arnold — 1827 — 1901 — Swiss
Swiss painter
Famous Works: The Island of the
Dead

Manet, Edouard — 1832 — 1883 — French
Open Air Depictions/Balcony
Outraged French Academy

	Born	Died	Nationality
Whistler, James Abbot McNeill Japanese manner/Nocturne in Blue and Gold	1834	1903	American
Degas, Edgar Actuality/Cafe Concert/Theatrical Effects	1834	1917	French
Cezanne, Paul Father of Modern Art/Mont Sainte- Victoire/Formulated What He Saw	1839	1906	French
Rodin, Auguste Sculptor/Impressionistic The Hand of God/Acknowledged Master	1840	1917	French
Monet, Claude Impressionistic/Regatta/Painted Effect of Light Outdoors	1840	1926	French
Renoir, Pierre Auguste Impressionist Nude/Painted Contemporary Life	1841	1919	French
Morisot, Berthe Impressionist Cradle/Student of Manet	1841	1895	French
Cassatt, Mary Impressionist	1844	1926	American
Gauguin, Paul Symbolist/Riders on the Beach/Lived in Tahiti	1848	1903	French
Gogh, Vincent van Patron Saint of Modern Art Sunflowers/rejected genius	1853	1890	Dutch
Matisse, Henri Modern The Persian Dress/Master of Colour	1869	1954	French
Klee, Paul Intellectual/Polyphony/Perceptual Analyst	1879	1940	Swiss
Epstein, Sir Jacob Vorticist/Rock Drill	1880	1959	English
Picasso, Pablo Ruiz y Cubist/Guitar with fruit-dish and grapes Originated Cubist Movement	1881	1973	Spanish
Braque, Georges Cubist/The Paleme	1882	1963	French

	Born	Died	Nationality
Nash, Paul	1889	1946	English
Surrealism – official war artist			
Spencer, Sir Stanley	1891	1959	English
Modern Painter			
Famous Works: Resurrection of the Soldiers			
Sutherland, Graham	1903	1980	British
Romantic Painter			
Famous Works: Christ in Glory, Tapestry			
Dali, Salvador	1904	–	Spanish
Surrealist			
Mae West/Dream Spaces			

CHAPTER FIVE

COMPOSERS

	Born	Died	Nationality	Era
Philippe de Vitry	1291	1361	French	Middle Ages

Style: Secular and of the
Arts Nova
Famous works:
Impudenter circumivi/
Virtutibus

	Born	Died	Nationality	Era
Guillaume de Machant	1300	1377	French Reims	Middle Ages

Style: Sacred and secular
Famous works: Messe de
Notre Dame
Notes: Well respected
statesman, cleric and
poet

	Born	Died	Nationality	Era
Francesco Landini	1325	1397	Italian	Middle Ages

Style: Secular
Famous works: Ecco la
primavera
Notes: Blind from
childhood

	Born	Died	Nationality	Era
John Dunstable	1390	1453	English	Middle Ages

Style: Sacred and secular
Famous works: O Rosa
Bella
Notes: Well known for
'singability' of his music

	Born	Died	Nationality	Era
Guillaume Dufay	1400	1460	French	Renaissance

Style: Sacred and secular
Famous works: Se la face
aypale

	Born	Died	Nationality	Era
Gilles de Bins (Binchois) Style: Sacred and secular Famous works: Filles a marier	1400	1460	Franco-Flemish	Renaissance
Johannes Ockeghem Style: Sacred and secular Famous works: Missa cuiusvi toni	1410	1497	Franco-Flemish	Renaissance
Josquin Desprez Style: Sacred and secular Famous works: Ave Maria	1440	1521	French	Renaissance
Heinrich Isaac Style: Secular Famous works: Choralis constantinus	1450	1517	Flemish	Renaissance
Andrea Gabrieli Style: Sacred and madrigals Notes: Introduced technique 'Cori spezzati' (spaced choirs)	1510	1586	Italian/Venice	Renaissance
Giovanni Pierluigi da Palestrina Style: Sacred and secular vocal music Famous works: Missa Papae Marcelli	1525	1594	Italian/nr Rome	Renaissance
Orlande de Lassus Style: Sacred and secular vocal music Famous works: Alma redemptoris mater	1532	1594	Franco-Flemish	Renaissance
William Byrd Style: Sacred choral music, vocal chamber music, instrumental and	1543	1623	British	Renaissance

keyboard music
Famous works: Sing
Joyfully/Ave Verum
Corpus
Notes: Described as
Father of British Music

	Born	Died	Nationality	Era
Guilio Caccini Style: Le Nuove Musiche	1545	1618	Italian	Baroque
Tomas Luis de Victoria Style: Sacred vocal music Famous works: Mass Laetatus Sum	1548	1611	Spanish	Renaissance
Luca Marenzio Style: Secular vocal music and sacred vocal music Famous works: Dolorosi martir	1553	1599	Italian	Renaissance
Giovanni Gabrieli Style: Sacred vocal music, instrumental music and secular vocal music Famous works: Canzon XIII	1555	1612	Italian	Renaissance
Thomas Morley Style: Ballett (light form of madrigal) Famous works: Now is the month of maying	1557	1602	English	Renaissance
Carlo Gesualdo	1560	1613		Renaissance
John Bull Style: Keyboard composer Famous works: Fantasia, Canzona	1562	1628	British	Renaissance

41

	Born	Died	Nationality	Era
John Dowland	1563	1626	English	Renaissance

Style: Secular vocal,
sacred vocal,
instrumental music
Famous works: In
darknesse, Let mee
dwell, Flow my teares

	Born	Died	Nationality	Era
Claudio Monteverdi	1567	1643	Italian	Baroque

Style: Secular vocal,
sacred vocal, madrigals,
operas
Famous works:
Madrigals of Love and
War, Il ritorno d'Ulisse
in patria (The return of
Ulysses to his country)

	Born	Died	Nationality	Era
Thomas Weelkes	1575	1623	English	Renaissance

Style: Madrigals
Famous works: As Vesta
was from Latmos Hill
descending

	Born	Died	Nationality	Era
Orlando Gibbons	1583	1625	British	Renaissance

Style: Vocal and sacred
choral

	Born	Died	Nationality	Era
Girolamo Frescobaldi	1583	1643	Italian	Baroque

Style: Secular and sacred,
mostly vocal works
Notes: Known as 'A
giant among organists'

	Born	Died	Nationality	Era
Heinrich Schutz	1585	1672	German	Baroque

Style: Secular vocal
music
Famous works: St.
Matthew's Passion,
Christmas Oratorio

	Born	Died	Nationality	Era
Francesco Cavalli	1602	1676	Italian	Baroque

Style: Secular vocal
Famous works: Ercole

	Born	Died	Nationality	Era
Amante (Hercules the Lover)				

Giacomo Carissimi
Style: Sacred musical dramas
Famous works: The Representation of the Body and Soul

	Born	Died	Nationality	Era
	1605	1674	Italian	Baroque

Jean-Baptiste Lully
Style: Sacred choral music, comedy ballet, operas, ballets and dance music
Famous works: L'amour medecin

	Born	Died	Nationality	Era
	1632	1687	Italian	Baroque

Dietrich Buxtehude
Style: Oratorios, cantatas, arias
Notes: Began idea of evening music, public concerts in churches and known as great influence to Bach

	Born	Died	Nationality	Era
	1637	1707	Danish	Baroque

Arcangelo Corelli
Style: Church sonatas
Famous works: Christmas Concerto

	Born	Died	Nationality	Era
	1653	1713	Italian	Baroque

Henry Purcell
Style: Secular and sacred choral music, instrumental and keyboard music
Famous works: My heart is inditing, Fantasia upon One Note

	Born	Died	Nationality	Era
	1659	1695	British	Baroque

Alessandro Scarlatti
Style: Sacred and secular, choral and vocal music,

	Born	Died	Nationality	Era
	1660	1725	Italian	Baroque

	Born	Died	Nationality	Era
operas, instrumental music
Famous works: Le Teodora augusta				
Francois Couperin
Style: Keyboard music especially harpsichord, chamber music, sacred vocal music
Famous works: Concerts Royaux	1668	1733	French	Baroque
Antonio Vivaldi
Style: Concertos, operas, sacred choral music and chamber music
Famous works: Four Seasons	1678	1741	Italian	Baroque
Georg Philipp Telemann
Style: Progressive composer
Famous works: Musique de table	1681	1767	German	Baroque
Jean-Philippe Rameau
Style: Operas, keyboard music, chamber music and sacred choral music
Famous works: Hippolyte et Aricie	1683	1764	French	Baroque
Johann Sebastian Bach
Style: Sacred choral, secular vocal, orchestral chamber music, keyboard music, organ music
Famous works: St. John's Passion, The Well-tempered Keyboard	1685	1750	German	Baroque

	Born	Died	Nationality	Era
George Frederic Handel	1685	1759	German	Baroque

Style: Operas, oratorios,
sacred vocal, secular
vocal, orchestral,
chamber music and
keyboard music
Famous works: Water
Music, Music for Royal
Fireworks

	Born	Died	Nationality	Era
Domenico Scarlatti	1685	1757	Italian	Baroque

Style: Keyboard, sacred
choral, instrumental
and operas

	Born	Died	Nationality	Era
Christoph Willibald Gluck	1714	1787	Erasbach	Classical

Style: Operas, ballet,
songs, sacred vocal music
and chamber music
Famous works: Don
Juan, Orfeo ed Euridice

	Born	Died	Nationality	Era
Carl Philipp Emanuel Bach	1714	1788	German	Classical

Style: Keyboard,
orchestral, chamber and
choral music
Famous works: Rondo in
E Flat

	Born	Died	Nationality	Era
Franz Joseph Haydn	1732	1809	Austrian	Classical

Style: Symphonies,
chamber music, operas,
oratorios, choral music
Famous works: Sturm
und Drang

	Born	Died	Nationality	Era
Johann Christian Bach	1735	1782	German	Classical

Style: Orchestral,
chamber, keyboard,
operas and sacred music

	Born	Died	Nationality	Era
Luigi Boccherini Style: Chamber music, symphonies and concertos	1743	1805	Lucca	Classical
Muzio Clementi Style: Composed for piano Notes: Known as 'Father of pianoforte'	1752	1832	Austrian/ French	Classical
Wolfgang Amadeus Mozart Style: Operas, symphonies, concertos, choral music, chamber music, piano music, vocal music Famous works: The Magic Flute, Don Giovanni	1756	1791	Austrian	Classical
Ignace Peeyel	1757	1831		
Ludwig van Beethoven Styles: Symphonies, concertos, choral music, piano music, string quartet, chamber music, songs Famous works: Pastoral Symphony, Fidelio	1770	1827	German	Classical
Carl Maria von Weber Style: Operas, orchestral music, choral music, piano music, incidental music Famous works: The Freeshooter, Invitation to the Dance	1786	1826	German	Romantic
Gioachino Rossini Style: Operas, sacred	1792	1868	Italian	Romantic

46

choral music, secular and
chamber music
Famous works: Barber of
Seville, William Tell

	Born	*Died*	*Nationality*	*Era*
Franz Schubert	1797	1828	Austrian Vienna	Romantic

Style: Songs, orchestral,
chamber, piano and
operas
Famous works: Beautiful
Maid of the Mill, The
Trout
Notes: Died when only
31 years old

Vincenzo Bellini	1801	1865	Italian	Romantic

Style: Vocal

Hector Berlioz	1803	1869	French	Romantic

Style: Opera, orchestral
symphonies, sacred
choral music, secular
choral music, vocal music
Famous works:
Symphonie Fantastique,
Romeo et Juliette

Felix Mendelssohn	1809	1847	German	Romantic

Style: Orchestral music
symphonies, chamber
music, piano music,
sacred choral music
Famous works: A
Midsummer Nights
Dream, The Hebrides

Robert Schumann	1810	1856	Zwichau	Romantic

Style: Song, piano music,
orchestral, chamber,
opera and choral music
Famous works: A
Woman's Love and Life,
Scenes from Faust

	Born	Died	Nationality	Era
Frederic Chopin Style: Piano music, orchestral music, chamber music Famous works: The Etudes	1810	1849	Warsaw	Romantic
Franz Liszt Style: Orchestral music, piano music, choral music Famous works: The Hungarian Rhapsodies, Faust Symphony	1811	1886	Hungarian	Romantic
Richard Wagner Style: Operas, orchestral music, songs Famous works: The Flying Dutchman	1813	1883	German	Romantic
Giuseppe Verdi Style: Operas, sacred choral, secular choral, chamber music Famous works: Rigoletto, Requiem	1813	1901	Italian	Romantic
Bedrich Smetana Style: Symphonic poems and opera Famous works: The Bartered Bride, Vltava	1824	1884	Czechoslovak	Turn of Century
Anton Bruckner Style: Symphonies, choral music, chamber music Famous works: Te Deum	1824	1896	Vienna	Turn of Century
Johannes Brahms Style: Orchestral, chamber music, piano music, choral music	1833	1897	German	Romantic

	Born	Died	Nationality	Era

Famous works:
Hungarian Dances,
Tragic Overture, German
Requiem

Alexander Borodin — 1833 1887 Russian — Turn of Century
Style: Symphonies and
operas
Famous works: Prince
Igor

Modest Mussorgsky — 1839 1881 Russian — Turn of Century
Style: Operas, orchestral,
songs and piano music
Famous works: The
Nursery, Sun Less

Pyotr Ilyich — 1840 1893 Russian — Turn of Century
Tchaikovsky
Style: Operas, ballet,
choral music,
symphonies, chamber
music
Famous works: Sleeping
Beauty, The Nutcracker

Antonin Dvorak — 1841 1904 Czechoslovak — Turn of Century
Style: Orchestral musical
symphonies, operas,
chamber music
Famous works: From the
New World, The
American

Nikolay Rimsky- — 1844 1908 Russian — Turn of Century
Korsakov
Style: Operas, orchestral
works
Famous works: Snow
Maiden

Leos Janacek — 1854 1928 Czechoslovak — Turn of Century
Style: Operas, choral,
vocal, orchestral music,

	Born	Died	Nationality	Era
chamber music Famous works: The Bartered Bride, The Cunning Little Vixen				
Edward Elgar Style: Orchestral, choral, chamber, songs, piano, incidental Famous works: Pomp & Circumstance, original theme Enigma, The Apostles	1857	1934	British	Turn of Century
Giacomo Puccini Style: Operas, choral music, instrumental Famous works: La Boheme, Madame Butterfly	1858	1924	Italian	Turn of Century
Hugo Wolf Style: Songs, opera Famous works: Der Corregidor	1860	1903	Vienna	Turn of Century
Gustav Mahler Style: Symphonies, songs, choral music Famous works: The Resurrection, Songs of the Wayfarer, The Boy's Magic Horn	1860	1911	Vienna	Turn of Century
Claude Debussy Style: Orchestral, operas, ballet, piano, chamber music Famous works: Afternoon of the Faun, La Mer	1862	1918	French	Turn of Century
Richard Strauss Style: Orchestral, operas,	1864	1949	German	Turn of Century

choral music, song
Famous works: The
Cavalier of the Rose, A
Woman without a
Shadow

	Born	Died	Nationality	Era
Jean Sibelius	1865	1957	Finnish	Turn of Century

Style: Orchestral,
incidental, choral,
chamber
Famous works: Tone
Poem en Saga, Nightride
and Sunrise, The
Tempest

	Born	Died	Nationality	Era
Ralph Vaughan Williams	1872	1958	British	Modern Times

Style: Operas, ballets,
orchestral music,
incidental, vocal,
chamber music
Famous works: The
Pilgrim's Progress,
Pastoral Symphony,
Fantasia on Greensleeves

	Born	Died	Nationality	Era
Sergey Rachmaninov	1873	1943	Russian	Turn of Century

Style: Orchestral, piano
and choral
Famous works:
Rhapsody on a Theme of
Paganini for Piano and
Orchestra, The Bells

	Born	Died	Nationality	Era
Charles Ives	1874	1954	American	Modern Times

Style: Orchestral, choral,
chamber and piano
Famous works: The
Circus Band, Three
Places in New England,
The Unanswered
Question

	Born	Died	Nationality	Era
Arnold Schoenberg Style: Operas, choral, orchestral, chamber and vocal Famous works: The Blessed Hand, The Transfigured Knight	1874	1951	Vienna	Modern Times
Maurice Ravel Style: Orchestral, piano, chamber music, song Famous works: Rapsodie Espagnole, Mother Goose	1875	1937	French	Turn of Century
Manuela de Falla Style: Opera Famous works: The Three Cornered Hat, Atlantida	1876	1946	Spanish	Modern Times
Bela Bartok Style: Operas, ballets, orchestral, chamber and piano music Famous works: Duke Bluebeard's Castle, The Wooden Prince, The Miraculous Mandarin	1881	1945	Hungarian	Modern Times
Igor Stravinsky Style: Operas, ballet, orchestral music, choral music Famous works: The Firebird, The Rite of Spring, Orpheus, The Soldier's Tale	1882	1971	Russian	Modern Times
Edgard Varese Style: Orchestral, vocal, instrumental and electronic Famous works: Ameriques, Hyperprism	1883	1965	French/American	Modern Times

	Born	Died	Nationality	Era
Anton Webern Style: Orchestral, choral, chamber and vocal Famous works: Passacaglia, Das Augenlicht	1883	1945	Vienna	Modern Times
Alban Berg Style: Opera, orchestral, chamber music, songs, piano music Famous works: Wozzeck, Lulu	1885	1935	Vienna	Modern Times
Louis Durey Style: Opera Notes: One of 'Les Six'	1888	1979	French	Modern Times
Sergey Prokofiev Style: Operas, ballets, orchestral, choral, chamber music Famous works: The Gambler, War and Peace, Romeo and Juliet	1891	1953	Ukranian	Modern Times
Germaine Tailleferre Style: Opera Notes: One of 'Les Six'	1892	1983	French	Modern Times
Darius Milhaud Style: Opera Notes: One of 'Les Six'	1892	1974	French	Modern Times
Arthur Honegger Style: Opera Notes: One of 'Les Six'	1892	1955	French	Modern Times
Paul Hindemith Style: Operas, ballets, orchestral, chamber, piano, organ, vocal, choral	1895	1963	German	Modern Times

	Born	Died	Nationality	Era
Famous works: Matthias
The Painter, The Four
Temperaments

Carl Orff 1895 1981 German Modern Times
Style: Cantatas
Famous works: Carmina
Burana

Henry Cowell 1897 1965 American Modern Times
Style: Orchestral,
instrumental, piano
Famous works:
Synchrony, Hymn &
Fuguing Tune, Mosaic

Georges Auric 1899 1983 French Modern Times
Style: Opera
Notes: One of 'Les Six'

Francis Poulenc 1899 1963 French Modern Times
Style: Opera
Famous Works: A Sonata
for Two clarinets,
Dialogue des Carmelites
Notes: Leader of 'Les
Six'

Kurt Weill 1900 1950 German Modern Times
Style: Opera, ballet,
orchestral, choral and
chamber
Famous works: The
Threepenny Opera, The
Nickerbocker Holiday,
The Rise and Fall of the
City of Mahagonny

Dmitry Shostakovich 1906 1975 Russian Modern Times
Style: Orchestral, operas,
chamber music and piano
Famous works: The First
of May, Leningrad, The
Nose

	Born	Died	Nationality	Era
Benjamin Britten	1913	1976	British	Modern Times

Style: Operas, church, orchestral, choral and chamber

Famous works: The Turn of the Screw, A Midsummer Nights Dream, Variations on a Theme of Frank Bridge, Spring Symphony

CHAPTER SIX

WRITERS

	Born	Died	Nationality

Geoffrey Chaucer — 1340 1400 British
Educated: London
Famous works: The Canterbury Tales
Notes: Known as the Father of English
Literature

Edmund Spenser — 1552 1599 British
Educated: Merchant Taylors School,
Northampton
Famous works: The Faerie Queene,
Colin Clouts Comes Home Againe
Notes: Writings closely associated with
the stages of his life

Sir Walter Raleigh — 1552 1618 British
Educated: Oxford (Law)
Famous works: The History of the
World, The Discoverie of the Large,
Rich and Beautiful Empyre of Guiana
Notes: Had an enquiring mind and an
uncommon literary ability

Francis Bacon — 1561 1626 British
Educated: Trinity College, Cambridge
(Law)
Famous works: The Advancement of
Learning
Notes: Had unquenchable curiosity
about nature of the World and
behaviour of his fellow men

William Shakespeare — 1564 1616 British
Educated: Holy Trinity Church,
Stratford
Famous works: Othello, King Lear,

Macbeth, Anthony and Cleopatra etc
Notes: Most prolific period 1604–1608.
It is said of him that 'he is not of an age
but for all time'

Christopher Marlowe　　　　1564 1593　British
Educated: Corpus Christi College,
Cambridge
Famous works: The Passionate
Shepherd
Notes: Died from stabbing during fight
with friends while gambling on
backgammon

Ben Jonson　　　　　　　　1572 1637　British
Educated: Westminster School
Famous works: Volpone,
Batholomew Fayre, Timber
Notes: Leader of new generation of
poets known as The Tribe of Ben

John Donne　　　　　　　　1572 1631　British
Educated: Oxford and Cambridge
Famous works: Devotions, Elegies
Notes: Greatest fame as a prose writer
of some 160 sermons

John Milton　　　　　　　　1608 1674　British
Famous works: Paradise Lost, On
His Blindness, Il Penseroso
Notes: The Civil War diverted his
energies to the parliamentary and
political struggle. Wrote Paradise Lost
and On His Blindness after he had
become blind

John Bunyan　　　　　　　　1628 1688　British
Educated: Village school, Elstow
Famous works: The Pilgrim's
Progress, Grace Abounding
Notes: Imprisoned for 12 years for
unlicenced preaching

John Dryden　　　　　　　　1631 1700　British
Educated: Westminster and Trinity

College, Cambridge
Famous works: Marriage a la Mode,
The Rehearsal
Notes: Poet Laureate in 1668

Samuel Pepys   1633 1703 British
Educated: St. Paul's School and
Magdalen College, Cambridge
Famous works: Diary
Notes: Diary discovered after his death

Daniel Defoe   1660 1731 British
Educated: Stoke Newington Academy
Famous works: Robinson Crusoe
Notes: Busiest most prolific time after
age of 60; known as founder of English
journalism

Jonathan Swift   1667 1754 British
Educated: Kilkenny School, Dublin
and Trinity College
Famous works: A Tale of a Tub,
Gulliver's Travels
Notes: From age 23 suffered from
Menieres Disease

Joseph Addison   1672 1719 British
Educated: Charterhouse School and
Magdalen College, Oxford
Famous works: Cato
Notes: Member of Parliament for all of
his life

George Berkeley   1685 1753 Irish
Educated: Trinity College, Dublin
Famous works: An Essay Towards a
New Theory of Vision, Alciphron
Notes: First published works were
tracts on Mathematics, written in Latin

Alexander Pope   1688 1744 British
Educated:Self-educated
Famous works: The Rape of the Lock
and translations of The Iliad and
Odyssey

Notes: Suffered from ill health most of his life

Samuel Richardson   1689 1761 British
Educated: Grew up in poverty, education sketchy
Famous works: Pamela, Clarissa
Notes: Obsessed with sex, which led to the popularity of his writing

Benjamin Franklin   1706 1790 American
Educated: Born Boston, education sketchy
Famous works: Observation on the relationships of Britain to her colonies, Rules by which a Great Empire may be reduced to a Small One
Notes: Founded the influential social and debating society (The Junto Club)

Henry Fielding   1707 1754 British
Educated: Eton
Famous works: Tom Thumb, The History of the Adventures of Joseph Andrews
Notes: Very sick much of his life with asthma and dropsy

Samuel Johnson   1709 1784 British
Educated: Pembroke College, Oxford
Famous works: The Vanity of Human Wishes
Notes: Recognised that pursuit of learning for its own sake was barren and that it needed to be related to the knowledge of life

Thomas Gray   1716 1771 British
Educated: Tutors and Peterhouse College, Cambridge
Famous works: Elegy written in a country churchyard
Notes: Letters are among finest in the language, incredible descriptive powers and wit

	Born	Died	Nationality

Tobias George Smollett   1721 1771 British
Educated: Dumbarton School and
Glasgow University
Famous works: The Expedition of
Humphrey Clinker, A Memorable
Prophecy of Doctor Smollett

Oliver Goldsmith   1728 1774 Irish
Educated: Trinity College, Dublin
Famous works: The Vicar of
Wakefield, She Stoops to Conquer, The
Citizen of the World
Notes: In his own words, he was mostly
addicted to gambling and was an
experienced liar

Edmund Burke   1729 1797 Irish
Educated: Quakers School, Balitore
and Trinity College, Dublin
Famous works: The Reflexions on the
Revolution in France
Notes: Founded The Annual Register

William Cowper   1731 1800 British
Educated: Westminster School, The
Inner Temple (Law)
Famous works: The Verses Supposed
To Be Written By Alexander Selkirk
Notes: Unwittingly gave poetry a new
direction

James Boswell   1740 1795 Scottish
Educated: Edinburgh University (Law)
Famous works: The Life of Dr Johnson
Notes: Felt thwarted because he did not
attain the political career he wanted

Fanny Burney   1752 1840 British
Self-educated
Famous works: Evelina, Cecilia,
Camilla
Notes: Her diary is one of the best
sources of first-hand portraits of late
18th century characters and life

60

	Born	Died	Nationality

George Crabbe — 1754, 1832, British
Educated: Apprentice to a doctor
Famous works: The Village

William Blake — 1757, 1827, British
Educated: Royal Academy at Somerset House
Famous works: Songs of Innocence and Experience, The Marriage of Heaven and Hell
Notes: Volumes of meaning expressed in apparently simple musical lines of his poetry

Robert Burns — 1759, 1796, Scottish
Educated: By his father and mother
Famous work: Tam-o'-Shanter, Auld Lang Syne
Notes: Wrote most remarkable cantata, The Jolly Beggar

William Cobbett — 1762, 1835, British
Educated: Self-educated in the Army
Famous works: Rural Rides, Cobbett's Political Register
Notes: His published output was enormous, from farming to politics

William Wordsworth — 1770, 1850, British
Educated: Hawkshead Grammar School and St John's College, Cambridge
Famous works: Sonnets, Ode on the Intimations of Immortality, Prelude
Notes: Achieved a remarkable expression of emotions that often lie submerged

Sir Walter Scott — 1771, 1832, Scottish
Educated: Royal High School and University in Edinburgh
Famous works: Ivanhoe, Kenilworth
Notes: Wrote almost 40 novels from 1814 to 1832

	Born	Died	Nationality
Samuel Taylor Coleridge	1772	1834	British

Samuel Taylor Coleridge
Educated: Jesus College, Cambridge
Famous works: Rime of the Ancient
Mariner, Kubla Khan
Notes: Gained knowledge of
physiology, anatomy and natural
history in Germany

Charles Lamb   1775 1834 British
Educated: Christ's Hospital
Famous works: Adventures of Ulysses,
Prince Doras, Essays of Elia
Notes: Devoted his life to his sister,
who was of unstable mind

Jane Austen   1775 1817 British
Educated: by her father
Famous works: Emma, Mansfield Park,
Pride and Prejudice
Notes: Portrayed middle-class society
with a remarkable subtlety

William Hazlitt   1778 1830 British
Educated: Hackney College, London
(Art and Metaphysics)
Famous works: The Characters of
Shakespeare's Plays
Notes: Ability as a critic with
remarkable physical descriptions
through his observant artistic eye

Thomas de Quincey   1785 1859 British
Educated: Manchester Grammar
School
Famous works: Confessions of an
Opium-eater
Notes: Addicted to opium; work of
uneven quality

Lord George Gordon Byron   1788 1824 British
Educated: Aberdeen Grammar School,
Harrow School, Trinity College,
Cambridge
Famous works: Manfred, Don Juan,

Childe Harold
Notes: Enormous influence on both
Europe and England

James Fenimore Cooper   1789 1851   American
Educated: Albany and Yale
Famous works: The Spy, The Last of
the Mohicans
Notes: A judge

Percy Bysshe Shelley   1792 1822   British
Educated: University College, Oxford
Famous works: Promethius Unbound
Notes: Died at 30 in a storm while
sailing

John Clare   1793 1864   British
Educated: by his father
Famous works: The Shepherd's
Calendar, Poems Descriptive of Rural
Life and Scenery
Notes: Known as the Peasant Poet,
spent much of his life in an asylum

John Keats   1795 1821   British
Educated: Harrow and Enfield
Academy
Famous works: Hyperion
Notes: Apprenticed to an apothecary,
qualified for study of surgery at Guys
Hospital. Extraordinary sensitivity to
the impression of the moment

Thomas Carlyle   1795 1881   Scottish
Educated: Annan Grammar School,
Edinburgh University
Famous works: Sartor Resartus
Notes: Lost the use of his right hand
and could no longer write

Elizabeth Barrett Browning   1806 1861   British
Educated: at home
Famous works: Cry of the Children,
Sonnets from the Portuguese, Aurora
Leigh

Notes: Married Robert Browning. She
was recommended as Poet Laureat

Henry Wadsworth Longfellow   1807 1882 American
Educated: Bowdoin, Portland Maine
Famous works: Hiawatha, The
Courtship of Miles Standish
Notes: First poems published at 13

Lord Alfred Tennyson   1809 1892 British
Educated: Louth Grammar School,
Trinity College Cambridge
Famous works: Maud, Crossing the Bar
Notes: Poet Laureat

Edgar Allan Poe   1809 1849 American
Educated: University of Virginia
Famous works: The Pit and the
Pendulum
Notes: Stories often weird and fantastic

William Makepeace Thackeray   1811 1863 British
Educated: Trinity College, Cambridge
(Law)
Famous works: Vanity Fair, The
Virginians
Notes: Travelled the U.S. Died at 52
from heartstrain

Charles Dickens   1812 1870 British
Intermittent education
Famous works: Pickwick Papers,
Oliver Twist
Notes: Often said he wrote about
himself in the character of Quilp, in
The Old Curiosity Shop. Died of a
stroke

Robert Browning   1812 1889 British
Educated: mostly at home
Famous works: The Ring and the Book
Notes: One of the great romances of
literary history with Elizabeth Barrett

	Born	Died	Nationality

Anthony Trollope
Educated: Harrow
Famous works: The Warden, Mr
Scarborough's Family, The Way We
Live Now
Notes: Clerk in the Post Office

1815 1882 British

Charlotte Brontë
Famous works: Jane Eyre
Notes: Taught in Brussels

1816 1855 British

Emily Brontë
Famous works: Wuthering Heights
Notes: Died of consumption

1818 1848 British

Walt Whitman
Educated: Brooklyn
Famous works: Leaves of Grass
Notes: Led a wandering life and did
hospital work in the Civil War

1819 1892 American

John Ruskin
Educated: by parents and
Christchurch, Oxford
Famous works: Modern Painters
Notes: Founded the Guild of St George

1819 1900 British

Charles Kingsley
Educated: King's College, London and
Magdalen College, Cambridge
Famous works: Westward Ho, The
Water Babies
Notes: Deeply concerned with social
reform but opposed to change brought
about by force

1819 1875 British

George Eliot
Famous works: Silas Mariner,
Middlemarch
Notes: Pseudonym for Mary Anne
Evans. Read extensively in Theology
and Languages

1819 1880 British

	Born	Died	Nationality
Anne Brontë	1820	1849	British

Famous works: Agnes Gray
Notes: Sometimes used pseudonym of
Acton Bell. Died of consumption

	Born	Died	Nationality
Matthew Arnold	1822	1888	British

Educated: Rugby and Balliol, Oxford
Famous works: The Scholar-Gipsy
Notes: Won Newdigate Prize for poetry
with Cromwell. Fellow of Oriel
College

	Born	Died	Nationality
Emily Dickinson	1830	1886	American

Notes: America's greatest woman poet,
always wrote in secret and after her
death it was discovered she had written
over 1700 poems. Her work is
considered technically insufficient but
flavour of the poetry appreciated

	Born	Died	Nationality
Lewis Carroll	1832	1898	British

Educated: Rugby School and Oxford
(Maths)
Famous works: Alice Through the
Looking Glass, Alice in Wonderland
Notes: Real name Charles Lutwidge
Dodgson, a lecturer in Mathematics at
Oxford

	Born	Died	Nationality
Mark Twain	1835	1910	American

Educated: Left school at 12
Famous works: Tom Sawyer,
Huckleberry Finn
Notes: Real name Samuel Langhorne
Clemens

	Born	Died	Nationality
Algernon Charles Swinburne	1837	1909	British

Educated: Eton and Balliol College,
Oxford
Famous works: Atalanta in Calydon,
Aeschylus and Sappho
Notes: His poetry often shocked

	Born	Died	Nationality

Thomas Hardy
Educated:
Famous works: Under the Greenwood
Tree, Far From the Madding Crowd,
The Dynasts
Notes: Apprenticed to an architect, he
was a novelist and a poet

Thomas Hardy — 1840 1928 British

Henry James — 1843 1916 American
Educated: Private tutors and part Law
School
Famous works: The Turn of the Screw,
What Maisie Knew, The Wings of the
Dove
Notes: Travelled between Europe and
America and wrote stories to explain
gulf that divided the two cultures.
Prolific writer but sometimes difficult
for the reader to understand

Gerard Manley Hopkins — 1844 1889 British
Educated: Balliol College, Oxford
Famous works: The Wreck of the
Deutschland
Notes: Was an ordained priest and
professor of Greek at University of
Dublin. Died from typhoid. Felt
conflict between poetry and religious
calling

Oscar Wilde — 1854 1900 Irish
Educated: Portora Royal School,
Trinity College, Dublin and Magdalen
College, Oxford
Famous works: The Importance of
Being Earnest
Notes: Leader of the cult of art for art's
sake

George Bernard Shaw — 1856 1950 Irish
Educated: Day school left at 15
Famous works: The Widower's House,
Mrs Warren's Profession, Man and
Superman, Pygmalion

Notes: Became known as journalist and wrote nearly 60 plays. Letters edited by D. H. Lawrence

Joseph Conrad   1857 1924 British
Famous works: Lord Jim, Secret Agent, Under Western Eyes, Chance
Notes: Born Polish Ukraine but exiled. Master Mariner in British Merchant Service. Wrote with clarity but never learnt to speak English well. Moralist, was one of the most famous living authors

Sir Arthur Conan Doyle   1859 1930 British
Educated: Edinburgh University (Medicine)
Famous works: Sherlock Holmes
Notes: A doctor, wrote short stories to implement his income. Preferred to write historical romances. Defence of British policy in South Africa won him knighthood

J. M. Barrie   1860 1937 Scottish
Educated: by his mother, Dumfries Academy and Edinburgh University
Famous works: Peter Pan
Notes: The Boy David, his final work, awaits revival so that it can be properly judged in terms of the stage

William Butler Yeats   1865 1939 Irish
Educated: London, Art School
Famous works: Tables of Law, Adoration of the Magi
Notes: Encouraged by his father, his Celtic inheritance a powerful influence for him. Founded Dublin Hermetic Society to promote the study of oriental religions and theosophy. Fell in love with Maud Gonne but she refused to marry him – he continued to love her throughout his life. He married another

and they attempted 'automatic writing' with striking results

Rudyard Kipling   1865 1936 British
Educated: United Services College, Devon
Famous works: Love-O'-Women, Kim, Puck of Pook's Hill
Notes: Born Bombay, his family moved to London but he was abandoned when his parents returned to India. Kipling as a reporter wrote a great deal about soldiers in the barrack room or in battle

H. G. Wells   1866 1946 British
Educated: Normal School of Science, Kensington
Famous works: The Time Machine, Island of Dr Moreau, Wheels of Chance, Love and Mr Lewisham
Notes: Mixed scientific journalism with teaching. All inventions done before the twentieth century. Science fiction and fantasy stories side-by-side

John Galsworthy   1867 1933 British
Educated: Harrow School and New College, Oxford (Law)
Famous works: Forsyte Saga, The Silver Spoon, The Modern Comedy
Notes: Used pseudonym of John Sinjohn until after his fifth book. Wrote 31 full length plays

(Enoch) Arnold Bennett   1867 1931 British
Famous works: The Grand Babylon Hotel, Anna of the Five Towns, The Gates of Wrath
Notes: Went to work for his father, a solicitor, at 18. Became a journalist and then novelist. Prolific writer

Walter de la Mare   1873 1956 British
Educated: St Paul's Choir School

69

Famous works:
Notes: Pseudonym used, Walter
Ramal. Continued to write into his 80's.
A poet, a storyteller, a novelist, and a
writer for children. Saw no need to look
down at children protectively

William Somerset Maugham   1874 1965   British
Educated: Kings School, Canterbury
and St Thomas Hospital (Medicine)
Famous works: Liza of Lambeth, Of
Human Bondage
Notes: Storyteller of genius with a
sardonic view of human behaviour,
anti-romantic and mercilessly
observant, with an unrivalled skill in
realising the climax of a story

Gilbert Keith Chesterton   1874 1936   British
Educated: at home until Trinity
College, Cambridge
Famous works: The Napoleon of
Notting Hill, The Ballad of the White
Horse
Notes: An Ambassador at the Hague
and Secretary of State. Letters written
in English, French and Latin

John Masefield   1878 1967   British
Educated: Kings School, Warwickshire
Famous works: Salt-Water Ballads,
Reynard The Fox
Notes: Went to sea but ill health
determined him to become a writer

Edward Morgan Forster   1879 1970   British
Educated: Tonbridge School, Kings
College Cambridge
Famous works: The Longest Journey,
A Room with a View, Where Angels
Fear to Tread, Passage to India
Notes: Member of the Apostle Society.
Chicago Tribune thought the author
was a woman

	Born	Died	Nationality

James (Augustine Aloysius) Joyce — Born 1882, Died 1941, Nationality Irish
Educated: Jesuit School Kildare,
University College Dublin
Famous works: Ulysses, Finnegan's
Wake, Portrait of the Artist
Notes: Ulysses published in serial form
but was stopped as obscene material

Ezra (Weston Loomis) Pound — Born 1885, Died 1972, Nationality American
Educated: University of Pennsylvania
and Hamilton College, N.Y.
Famous works: The Spirit of Romance
Notes: Travelled to Europe and was
away from America for 40 years. Placed
in an asylum but was visited and
supported by most of the well known
writers and intellects of the time

David Herbert Lawrence — Born 1885, Died 1930, Nationality British
Educated: Nottingham High School
Famous works: The White Peacock,
Sons and Lovers, Lady Chatterley's
Lover
Notes: Tried to interpret emotion on a
deeper level of consciousness.
Disharmony of home and parents
strongly affected him

Edith Louise Sitwell — Born 1887, Died 1965, Nationality British
Educated: at home
Famous works: Facade (set to music by
William Walton), Gold Coast Customs
Notes: One of most celebrated of
English women, awarded four honorary
doctorates

Thomas Stearns Eliot — Born 1888, Died 1965, Nationality British
Educated: Harvard University and
Merton College, Oxford
Famous works: The Waste Land, The
Four Quarters
Notes: The term 'Old Possum' was
Ezra Pound's nickname for Eliot and
referred to his soft-footed circuitous

71

approach. Born in St Louis, Missouri, became British subject in 1927

(Arthur) Joyce (Lunel) Cary   1888 1957 British
Educated: Tonbridge Wells, Clifton
College, Trinity College Oxford
Famous works: Aissa Saved
Notes: With British Red Cross in the
Balkan Wars and a District Magistrate
in Nigeria. Wrote his first novel at 44

Ivy Compton-Burnett   1892 1969 British
Educated: Royal Holloway College,
University of London
Famous works: Pastors and Masters
Notes: Her books deal with family
relationships, objectively and
unsentimentally

John Boynton Priestley   1894 1984 British
Educated: Trinity College Cambridge
Famous works: The Good Companions,
Dangerous Corner
Notes: Wrote essays, literary criticisms,
travel, fiction, autobiography and over
40 plays

Francis Scott Key Fitzgerald   1896 1940 American
Educated: Newman School, New
Jersey, and Princeton
Famous works: This Side of Paradise,
The Great Gatsby
Notes: Ernest Hemingway helped him
to write The Great Gatsby in France

William Harrison Faulkner   1897 1962 American
Educated: University of Mississippi
Famous works: The Sound and the
Fury, As I Lay Dying
Notes: Won Pullitzer and Nobel Prizes.
His novels should be read by anyone
who wants to understand the grim and
complex era of American life

	Born	Died	Nationality

Ernest Miller Hemingway   1898 1961 American
Famous works: In Our Time, A
Farewell To Arms, For Whom the Bell
Tolls, The Old Man and the Sea
Notes: Completely dedicated to his
literary career. Several of the literary
greats of his time helped him to realise
his talents. Shot himself at home in
Idaho

Noel Pierce Coward   1899 1973 British
Educated: Italia Conti Academy –
trained for the stage
Famous works: Private Lives, On with
the Dance, Hay Fever
Notes: Sought after actor and successful
playwright. Stage sense unerring and
ear for spoken dialogue flawless

Evelyn (Arthur St John) Waugh   1903 1966 British
Educated: Lancing School, Hertford
College Oxford
Famous works: Vile Bodies, Brideshead
Revisited
Notes: Worked as a teacher and a
journalist

George Orwell   1903 1950 British
Educated: Eton College
Famous works: Animal Farm, 1984
Notes: With Indian Civil Police in
Burma, then returned to Europe as a
teacher. Vivid commentator on reality
of depravation and became increasingly
pessimistic about affairs at home and
abroad

(Henry) Graham Greene   1904   British
Educated: Balliol College Oxford
Famous works: The Heart of the
Matter, Brighton Rock
Notes: Novelist, journalist and
playwright

73

	Born	Died	Nationality
Cecil Day-Lewis	1904	1972	British

Educated: Sherborne School, Wadham
College, Oxford
Famous works: Beechen, Vigil and
other poems
Notes: Poet Laureate and critic. Under
pseudonym Nicholas Blake wrote 20
detective novels

	Born	Died	Nationality
Samuel Beckett	1906		Anglo/Irish

Educated: Trinity College, Dublin
Famous works: Malone Dies, How It
Is, Waiting for Godot
Notes: Made France his home. Nobel
Prize winner

CHAPTER SEVEN

SHAKESPEARE

1589–92	*1 Henry VI, 2 Henry VI, 3 Henry VI*
1592–93	*Richard III, The Comedy of Errors*
1593–94	*Titus Andronicus, The Taming of the Shrew*
1594–95	*The Two Gentlemen of Verona, Love's Labour's Lost, Romeo and Juliet*
1595–96	*Richard II, A Midsummer Night's Dream*
1596–97	*King John, The Merchant of Venice*
1597–98	*1 Henry IV, 2 Henry IV*
1598–99	*Much Ado About Nothing, Henry V*
1599–1600	*Julius Caesar, As You Like It*
1600–01	*Hamlet, The Merry Wives of Windsor*
1601–02	*Twelfth Night, Troilus and Cressida*
1602–03	*All's Well That Ends Well*
1604–05	*Measure For Measure, Othello*
1605–06	*King Lear, Macbeth*
1606–07	*Antony and Cleopatra*
1607–08	*Coriolanus, Timon of Athens*
1608–09	*Pericles*
1609–10	*Cymbeline*
1610–11	*Winter's Tale*
1611–12	*The Tempest*
1612–13	*Henry VIII*

The First Part of
KING HENRY THE SIXTH

DRAMATIS PERSONÆ

1 KING HENRY THE SIXTH

2 DUKE OF GLOUCESTER, *uncle to the King and Lord Protector*

3 DUKE OF BEDFORD, *uncle to the King and Regent of France*

4 HENRY BEAUFORT, BISHOP OF WINCHESTER, *great-uncle to the King, afterwards* CARDINAL

5 THOMAS BEAUFORT, DUKE OF EXETER, *great-uncle to the King*

6 JOHN BEAUFORT, EARL OF SOMERSET, *afterwards* DUKE

7 RICHARD PLANTAGENET, *son of Richard late Earl of Cambridge, afterwards* DUKE OF YORK

8 EARL OF WARWICK

9 EARL OF SALISBURY

10 WILLIAM DE LA POLE, EARL OF SUFFOLK

11 LORD TALBOT, *afterwards Earl of Shrewsbury*

12 JOHN TALBOT, *his son*

13 EDMUND MORTIMER, *Earl of March*

14 SIR JOHN FASTOLFE

15 SIR WILLIAM LUCY

16 SIR WILLIAM GLANSDALE

17 SIR THOMAS GARGRAVE

18 MAYOR OF LONDON

19 OFFICER *of the Mayor of London*

20 WOODVILE, *Lieutenant of the Tower*

21 VERNON, *of the White Rose or York faction*

22 BASSET, *of the Red Rose or Lancaster faction*

23 LAWYER

24 GAOLER

25 SIX MESSENGERS

26 TWO WARDERS

27 THREE SERVANTS *to Gloucester*

28 SERVANT *to Talbot*

29 ENGLISH CAPTAIN

30 CAPTAIN *of Talbot's Army*

31 ENGLISH SOLDIER

32 CHARLES, *Dauphin, and afterwards King, of France*

33 REIGNIER, *Duke of Anjou and Maine, and titular King of Naples and Jerusalem*

34 DUKE OF BURGUNDY

35 DUKE OF ALENÇON

36 BASTARD OF ORLEANS

37 GOVERNOR OF PARIS

38 MASTER-GUNNER *of Orleans*

39 BOY *of Master-Gunner*

40 GENERAL *of the French Forces in Bourdeaux*

41 FRENCH SERGEANT

42 FRENCH SENTINEL

43 PORTER

44 SHEPHERD, *father to Joan La Pucelle*

45 FRENCH SOLDIER

46 WATCHMAN *of Rouen*

47 FRENCH SCOUT

48 PAPAL LEGATE

49 MARGARET, *daughter to Reignier, afterwards married to King Henry*

50 COUNTESS OF AUVERGNE

51 JOAN LA PUCELLE, *commonly called Joan of Arc*

52 NON-SPEAKING: *French Herald, Ambassadors, Soldiers, Gaolers, Servingmen, Attendants, and Fiends appearing to Joan La Pucelle*

The Second Part of
KING HENRY THE SIXTH

DRAMATIS PERSONÆ

1 KING HENRY THE SIXTH
2 HUMPHREY, DUKE OF
   GLOUCESTER, *his uncle*
3 CARDINAL BEAUFORT, BISHOP OF
   WINCHESTER *great-uncle to the*
   King
4 RICHARD PLANTAGENET, DUKE
   OF YORK
5 EDWARD   *sons of the*
6 RICHARD   *Duke of York*
7 DUKE OF SOMERSET
8 WILLIAM DE LA POLE,
   DUKE OF SUFFOLK
9 DUKE OF BUCKINGHAM   *King's*
10 LORD CLIFFORD   *Party*
11 YOUNG CLIFFORD, *his son*
12 EARL OF SALISBURY   *York*
13 EARL OF WARWICK   *Faction*
14 LORD SCALES
15 LORD SAY
16 SIR HUMPHREY STAFFORD
17 WILLIAM STAFFORD, *his brother*
18 SIR JOHN STANLEY
19 VAUX
20 SEA-CAPTAIN
21 MASTER
22 MASTER'S MATE
23 WALTER WHITMORE
24 TWO GENTLEMEN, *prisoners with*
   Suffolk
25 JOHN HUME
26 JOHN SOUTHWELL   *priests*
27 BOLINGBROKE, *a conjurer*
28 THOMAS HORNER, *an armourer*
29 PETER THUMP, *his man*
30 CLERK *of Chatham*

31 MAYOR *of Saint Alban's*
32 SIMPCOX, *an imposter*
33 ALEXANDER IDEN, *a Kentish*
   gentleman
34 JACK CADE, *a rebel*
35 GEORGE BEVIS
36 JOHN HOLLAND
37 DICK, *the butcher*   *followers*
38 SMITH, *the weaver*   *of Cade*
39 MICHAEL
40 TWO MURDERERS
41 FIVE MESSENGERS
42 TWO PETITIONERS
43 SPIRIT
44 BEADLE
45 TWO 'PRENTICES
46 THREE NEIGHBOURS TO HORNER
47 SERVANT *to Gloucester*
48 SHERIFF
49 HERALD
50 A POST
51 COMMONS
52 A CITIZEN
53 A SOLDIER
54 MARGARET, *Queen to King*
   Henry
55 ELEANOR, *Duchess of Gloucester*
56 MARGARET JOURDAIN, *a witch*
57 WIFE *to Simpcox*
58 NON-SPEAKING: *Mathew Goffe,*
   Petitioners, Guards, Servants,
   Attendants, Citizens,
   'Prentices, Officers of the
   Sheriff, Lords, Ladies, and
   Soldiers

The Third Part of
KING HENRY THE SIXTH

DRAMATIS PERSONÆ

1 KING HENRY THE SIXTH
2 EDWARD, PRINCE OF WALES,
    his son
3 LEWIS XI, *King of France*
4 DUKE OF SOMERSET
5 DUKE OF EXETER
6 EARL OF OXFORD
7 EARL OF NORTHUMBERLAND
8 EARL OF WESTMORLAND
9 LORD CLIFFORD
10 RICHARD PLANTAGENET, DUKE
    OF YORK
11 EDWARD, *Earl of March,*
    afterwards KING
    EDWARD IV
12 EDMUND, *Earl of Rutland* *his*
13 GEORGE, *afterwards* DUKE *sons*
    OF CLARENCE
14 RICHARD, *afterwards* DUKE
    OF GLOUCESTER
15 DUKE OF NORFOLK
16 MARQUESS OF MONTAGUE
17 EARL OF WARWICK
18 EARL OF PEMBROKE
19 LORD HASTINGS
20 LORD STAFFORD
21 SIR JOHN MORTIMER *uncles to*
22 SIR HUGH MORTIMER *the Duke*
    of York

23 LORD RIVERS, *brother to Lady*
    Grey
24 SIR WILLIAM STANLEY
25 SIR JOHN MONTGOMERY
26 SIR JOHN SOMERVILLE
27 TUTOR TO RUTLAND
28 MAYOR OF YORK
29 LIEUTENANT OF THE TOWER
30 NOBLEMAN
31 TWO KEEPERS
32 HUNTSMAN
33 SON, *that has killed his father*
34 FATHER, *that has killed his son*
35 SEVEN MESSENGERS
36 POST
37 SOLDIER
38 QUEEN MARGARET
39 ELIZABETH WOODVILLE, LADY
    GREY, *afterwards* QUEEN *to*
    Edward IV
40 BONA, *sister to the French Queen*

41 NON-SPEAKING: *Henry, Earl of*
    Richmond, Mayor of
    Coventry, Admiral called
    Bourbon, Nurse; Aldermen,
    Soldiers, Attendants

The Tragedy of
KING RICHARD THE THIRD

DRAMATIS PERSONÆ

1 KING EDWARD THE FOURTH
2 EDWARD, PRINCE OF WALES, *afterwards* KING EDWARD V, *later as a* GHOST *sons to the King*
3 RICHARD, DUKE OF YORK, *later as a* GHOST
4 GEORGE, DUKE OF CLARENCE, *later as a* GHOST *brothers to the King*
5 RICHARD, DUKE OF GLOUCESTER, *afterwards* KING RICHARD III
6 EDWARD, EARL OF WARWICK, *son of Clarence*
7 HENRY, EARL OF RICHMOND, *afterwards* KING HENRY VII
8 CARDINAL BOURCHIER, ARCHBISHOP OF CANTERBURY
9 THOMAS ROTHERHAM, ARCHBISHOP OF YORK
10 JOHN MORTON, BISHOP OF ELY
11 DUKE OF BUCKINGHAM, *later as a* GHOST
12 DUKE OF NORFOLK
13 EARL OF SURREY, *his son*
14 EARL RIVERS, *brother to Elizabeth, later as a* GHOST
15 MARQUIS OF DORSET
16 LORD GREY, *later as a* GHOST *sons to Elizabeth*
17 EARL OF OXFORD
18 LORD HASTINGS, *later as a* GHOST
19 LORD STANLEY, *later* EARL OF DERBY
20 LORD LOVEL

21 SIR THOMAS VAUGHAN, *later as a* GHOST
22 SIR RICHARD RATCLIFF
23 SIR WILLIAM CATESBY
24 SIR JAMES TYRREL
25 SIR JAMES BLUNT
26 SIR WALTER HERBERT
27 SIR ROBERT BRAKENBURY, *Lieutenant of the Tower*
28 CHRISTOPHER URSWICK, *a priest*
29 LORD MAYOR OF LONDON
30 SHERIFF OF WILTSHIRE
31 GENTLEMAN MOURNER
32 TWO MURDERERS
33 THREE CITIZENS
34 SIX MESSENGERS
35 PURSUIVANT
36 PRIEST
37 SCRIVENER
38 PAGE *to Richard III*
39 GHOSTS OF KING HENRY VI
40 LORDS
41 ELIZABETH, *queen to King Edward IV*
42 MARGARET, *widow of King Henry VI*
43 DUCHESS OF YORK, *mother to King Edward IV*
44 LADY ANNE, *widow of Edward Prince of Wales, son to King Henry VI, afterwards married to Richard, later as a* GHOST
45 MARGARET PLANTAGENET, *daughter of Clarence*
46 NON-SPEAKING: *Lords and other attendants, Two Bishops, Sir William Brandon, Citizens, Soldiers*

THE COMEDY OF ERRORS

DRAMATIS PERSONÆ

1 SOLINUS, DUKE OF EPHESUS
2 ÆGEON, *a merchant of Syracuse*
3 ANTIPHOLUS OF   *twin brothers,*
  EPHESUS   *and sons of*
4 ANTIPHOLUS OF   *Ægeon and*
  SYRACUSE   *Æmilia*
5 DROMIO OF   *twin brothers,*
  EPHESUS   *and attendants on*
6 DROMIO OF   *the two*
  SYRACUSE   *Antipholuses*
7 BALTHAZAR, *a merchant*
8 ANGELO, *a goldsmith*
9 FIRST MERCHANT, *friend to*
  Antipholus of Syracuse
10 SECOND MERCHANT, *to whom*
  Angelo is a debtor

11 PINCH, *a schoolmaster*
12 A SERVANT
13 A GAOLER
14 AN OFFICER
15 ÆMILIA, *wife to Ægeon, an*
  abbess at Ephesus
16 ADRIANA, *wife to Antipholus of*
  Ephesus
17 LUCIANA, *her sister*
18 LUCE, *servant to Adriana*
19 A COURTEZAN
20 NON-SPEAKING: *Officers and*
  other Attendants

TITUS ANDRONICUS

DRAMATIS PERSONÆ

1 SATURNINUS, *oldest son to the*
  late Emperor of Rome, and
  afterwards declared EMPEROR
2 BASSIANUS, *brother to*
  Saturninus; in love with
  Lavinia
3 TITUS ANDRONICUS, *a noble*
  Roman, general against the
  Goths
4 MARCUS ANDRONICUS, *tribune of*
  the people and brother to Titus
5 LUCIUS
6 QUINTUS   *sons to Titus*
7 MARTIUS   *Andronicus*
8 MUTIUS
9 YOUNG LUCIUS, *a boy, son to*
  Lucius
10 PUBLIUS, *son to Marcus the*
  tribune
11 ÆMILIUS, *a noble Roman*

12 DEMETRIUS   *sons to Tamora*
13 CHIRON
14 AARON, *a Moor, beloved by*
  Tamora
15 A CAPTAIN
16 A TRIBUNE
17 A MESSENGER
18 A CLOWN
19 THREE GOTHS
20 TAMORA, *Queen of the Goths*
21 LAVINIA, *daughter to Titus*
  Andronicus
22 A NURSE
23 NON-SPEAKING: *Sempronius,*
  Caius, and Valentine,
  kinsmen to Titus; Alarbus,
  oldest son to Tamora; Senators,
  Tribunes, Soldiers,
  Attendants, Romans, and
  Goths

THE TAMING OF THE SHREW

DRAMATIS PERSONÆ

1	A LORD	18	GRUMIO
2	CHRISTOPHER SLY, *a tinker*	19	CURTIS
		20	PETER
3	TWO HUNTSMEN	21	NATHANIEL
4	SERVINGMAN	22	PHILIP
5	PAGE	23	JOSEPH
6	MESSENGER	24	NICHOLAS
7	THREE SERVANTS	25	A PEDANT
8	PLAYERS	26	A TAILOR
9	HOSTESS	27	A HABERDASHER
10	BAPTISTA MINOLA, *a rich gentleman of Padua*	28	KATHARINA, *the shrew*
11	VINCENTIO, *an old gentleman of Pisa*	29	BIANCA
		30	WIDOW
12	LUCENTIO, *son to Vincentio, in love with Bianca*	31	NON-SPEAKING: *Attendants and servants*
13	PETRUCHIO, *a gentleman of Verona, a suitor to Katharina*		
14	GREMIO		
15	HORTENSIO		
16	TRANIO		
17	BIONDELLO		

Persons in the Induction (4, 5)

servants to Petruchio (21, 22)

daughters to Baptista (28, 29)

suitors to Bianca (14, 15)

servants to Lucentio (16, 17)

THE TWO GENTLEMEN OF VERONA

DRAMATIS PERSONÆ

1	DUKE OF MILAN, *Father to Silvia*	9	SPEED, *a clownish servant to Valentine*
2	VALENTINE	10	LAUNCE, *the like to Proteus*
3	PROTEUS	11	PANTHINO, *Servant to Antonio*
4	ANTONIO, *Father to Proteus*	12	JULIA, *beloved of Proteus*
5	THURIO, *a foolish rival to Valentine*	13	SILVIA, *beloved of Valentine*
6	EGLAMOUR, *Agent for Silvia in her escape*	14	LUCETTA, *waiting-woman to Julia*
7	HOST, *where Julia lodges*	15	NON-SPEAKING: *Servants and musicians*
8	THREE OUTLAWS, *with Valentine*		

the two Gentlemen (2, 3)

LOVE'S LABOUR'S LOST

DRAMATIS PERSONÆ

1 FERDINAND, KING OF NAVARRE
2 BIRON
3 LONGAVILLE   *lords attending on the King*
4 DUMAIN
5 BOYET   *lords attending on the Princess of France*
6 MERCADE
7 DON ADRIANO DE ARMADO, *a fantastical Spaniard*
8 SIR NATHANIEL, *a curate*
9 HOLOFERNES, *a schoolmaster*
10 DULL, *a constable*

11 COSTARD, *a clown*
12 MOTH, *a page to Armado*
13 A FORESTER
14 A LORD OF FRANCE
15 THE PRINCESS OF FRANCE
16 ROSALINE
17 MARIA   *ladies attending on the Princess*
18 KATHARINE
19 JAQUENETTA, *a country wench*
20 NON-SPEAKING: *Lords, Attendants, Blackamoors, etc.*

ROMEO AND JULIET

DRAMATIS PERSONÆ

1 ESCALUS, PRINCE OF VERONA
2 PARIS, *a young nobleman, kinsman to the Prince*
3 MONTAGUE
4 CAPULET   *heads of two houses at variance with each other*
5 COUSIN TO CAPULET, *an old man*
6 ROMEO, *son to Montague*
7 MERCUTIO, *kinsman to the Prince, and friend to Romeo*
8 BENVOLIO, *nephew to Montague, and friend to Romeo*
9 TYBALT, *nephew to Lady Capulet*
10 FRIAR LAURENCE
11 FRIAR JOHN   *Franciscans*
12 BALTHASAR, *servant to Romeo*
13 SAMPSON
14 GREGORY   *servants to Capulet*

15 PETER, *servant to Juliet's nurse*
16 ABRAHAM, *servant to Montague*
17 AN APOTHECARY
18 THREE MUSICIANS
19 PAGE *to Paris*
20 THREE WATCHMEN
21 A CITIZEN *of Verona*
22 THREE SERVANTS *to Capulet*
23 LADY MONTAGUE, *wife to Montague*
24 LADY CAPULET, *wife to Capulet*
25 JULIET, *daughter to Capulet*
26 NURSE *to Juliet*
27 CHORUS
28 NON-SPEAKING: *Citizens of Verona, Maskers, Musicians, Page to Mercutio, Guards, Watchmen, and Attendants*

The Tragedy of
KING RICHARD II
DRAMATIS PERSONÆ

1 KING RICHARD THE SECOND	15 LORD ROSS
2 JOHN OF GAUNT, DUKE OF LANCASTER *uncles to the*	16 LORD WILLOUGHBY
	17 LORD FITZWATER
	18 BISHOP OF CARLISLE
3 EDMUND OF LANGLEY, *King* DUKE OF YORK	19 ABBOT OF WESTMINSTER
	20 LORD MARSHAL
4 HENRY, *surnamed* BOLINGBROKE, DUKE OF HEREFORD, *son to John of Gaunt; afterwards* KING HENRY IV	21 SIR STEPHEN SCROOP
	22 SIR PIERCE OF EXTON
	23 CAPTAIN *to a band of Welshmen*
	24 TWO HERALDS
	25 ANOTHER LORD
5 DUKE OF AUMERLE, *son to the Duke of York*	26 GARDENER
	27 GROOM OF THE STABLE
6 THOMAS MOWBRAY, DUKE OF NORFOLK	28 KEEPER
	29 TWO SERVANTS *to York*
7 DUKE OF SURREY	30 SERVANT *to Exton*
8 EARL OF SALISBURY	31 QUEEN *to King Richard*
9 LORD BERKELEY	32 DUCHESS OF YORK
10 BUSHY	33 DUCHESS OF GLOUCESTER
11 BAGOT *servants to King Richard*	34 LADY *attending on the Queen*
12 GREEN	35 NON-SPEAKING: *Lords, Ladies, Officers, Soldiers, Gardeners, Guards, and other Attendants*
13 EARL OF NORTHUMBERLAND	
14 HENRY PERCY, *surnamed* Hotspur, *his son*	

A MIDSUMMER-NIGHT'S DREAM
DRAMATIS PERSONÆ

1 THESEUS, *Duke of Athens*	14 HELENA, *in love with Demetrius*
2 EGEUS, *father to Hermia*	15 OBERON, *King of the fairies*
3 LYSANDER *in love with Hermia*	16 TITANIA, *Queen of the fairies*
4 DEMETRIUS	17 PUCK, *or Robin Goodfellow*
5 PHILOSTRATE, *master of the revels to Theseus*	18 PEASEBLOSSOM
	19 COBWEB
6 QUINCE, *a carpenter*	20 MOTH *fairies*
7 SNUG, *a joiner*	21 MUSTARDSEED
8 BOTTOM, *a weaver*	22 TWO FAIRIES
9 FLUTE, *a bellows-mender*	23 NON-SPEAKING: *Attendants on Theseus and Hippolyta; fairies attending their King and Queen.*
10 SNOUT, *a tinker*	
11 STARVELING, *a tailor*	
12 HIPPOLYTA, *Queen of the Amazons, betrothed to Theseus*	
13 HERMIA, *daughter to Egeus, in love with Lysander*	

The Life and Death of
KING JOHN

DRAMATIS PERSONÆ

1 KING JOHN
2 PRINCE HENRY, *son to the King*
3 ARTHUR, *Duke of Bretagne,*
   nephew to the King
4 EARL OF PEMBROKE
5 EARL OF ESSEX
6 EARL OF SALISBURY
7 LORD BIGOT
8 HUBERT DE BURGH
9 ROBERT FAULCONBRIDGE, *son to*
   Sir Robert Faulconbridge
10 PHILIP THE BASTARD, *his half-*
   brother, later dubbed Richard
   Plantagenet
11 JAMES GURNEY, *servant to Lady*
   Faulconbridge
12 PETER OF POMFRET, *a prophet*
13 EXECUTIONER
14 TWO MESSENGERS
15 ENGLISH HERALD

16 PHILIP, *King of France*
17 LEWIS, *the Dauphin*
18 LYMOGES, DUKE OF AUSTRIA
19 CARDINAL PANDULPH, *the Pope's*
   legate
20 MELUN, *a French Lord*
21 CHATILLON, *ambassador from*
   France to King John
22 CITIZEN *of Angiers*
23 FRENCH HERALD
24 QUEEN ELINOR, *mother to King*
   John
25 CONSTANCE, *mother to Arthur*
26 BLANCH *of Spain, niece to King*
   John
27 LADY FAULCONBRIDGE
28 NON-SPEAKING: *Lords, Citizens*
   of Angiers, Sheriff, Officers,
   Soldiers and other Attendants

THE MERCHANT OF VENICE

DRAMATIS PERSONÆ

1 THE DUKE OF VENICE
2 PRINCE OF MOROCCO   *suitors to*
3 PRINCE OF ARRAGON   *Portia*
4 ANTONIO, *a merchant of Venice*
5 BASSANIO, *his friend, suitor*
   likewise to Portia
6 SALANIO
7 SALARINO   *friends to Antonio*
8 GRATIANO   *and Bassanio*
9 SALERIO
10 LORENZO, *in love with Jessica*
11 SHYLOCK, *a rich Jew*
12 TUBAL, *a Jew, his friend*
13 LAUNCELOT GOBBO, *the clown,*
   servant to Shylock

14 OLD GOBBO, *father to Launcelot*
15 LEONARDO, *servant to Bassanio*
16 BALTHASAR
17 STEPHANO   *servants to Portia*
18 SERVANT *to Antonio*
19 SERVANT *to Portia*
20 PORTIA, *a rich heiress*
21 NERISSA, *her waiting-maid*
22 JESSICA, *daughter to Shylock*
23 NON-SPEAKING: *Magnificoes of*
   Venice, Officers of the Court of
   Justice, Gaoler, Musicians,
   Servants to Portia, and other
   Attendants

The First Part of
KING HENRY THE FOURTH

DRAMATIS PERSONÆ

1 KING HENRY THE FOURTH

2 HENRY, PRINCE OF WALES

sons to the King

3 JOHN OF LANCASTER

4 EARL OF WESTMORELAND

5 SIR WALTER BLUNT

6 THOMAS PERCY, EARL OF WORCESTER

7 HENRY PERCY, EARL OF NORTHUMBERLAND

8 HENRY PERCY, *surnamed* HOTSPUR, *his son*

9 EDMUND MORTIMER, EARL OF MARCH

10 RICHARD SCROOP, ARCHBISHOP OF YORK

11 ARCHIBALD, EARL OF DOUGLAS

12 OWEN GLENDOWER

13 SIR RICHARD VERNON

14 SIR JOHN FALSTAFF

15 SIR MICHAEL, *a friend to the Archbishop of York*

16 POINS

17 GADSHILL

18 PETO

19 BARDOLPH

20 TWO CARRIERS

21 OSTLER

22 A CHAMBERLAIN

23 SEVERAL TRAVELLERS

24 A VINTNER

25 FRANCIS, *the drawer*

26 SHERIFF

27 TWO MESSENGERS

28 SERVANT *to Hotspur*

29 LADY PERCY, *wife to Hotspur, and sister to Mortimer*

30 LADY MORTIMER, *daughter to Glendower, and wife to Mortimer*

31 MISTRESS QUICKLY, *hostess of a tavern in Eastcheap*

32 NON-SPEAKING: *Lords, Officers, Drawers, Travellers and Attendants*

The Second Part of
KING HENRY THE FOURTH

DRAMATIS PERSONÆ

1 KING THE FOURTH

2 HENRY, PRINCE OF WALES, *afterwards* KING HENRY V

3 THOMAS, DUKE OF CLARENCE

his sons

4 PRINCE JOHN OF LANCASTER

5 PRINCE HUMPHREY OF GLOUCESTER

6 EARL OF WARWICK

7 EARL OF WESTMORELAND

8 GOWER

9 HARCOURT

10 LORD CHIEF JUSTICE *of the King's Bench*

11 A SERVANT *of the Chief Justice*

12 EARL OF NORTHUMBERLAND

13 SCROOP, ARCHBISHOP OF YORK

14 LORD MOWBRAY

15 LORD HASTINGS

16 LORD BARDOLPH

17 SIR JOHN COLEVILLE

18 TRAVERS *retainers of*

19 MORTON *Northumberland*

20 SIR JOHN FALSTAFF

85

21	PAGE *to Falstaff*	38	A MESSENGER
22	BARDOLPH	39	A BEADLE
23	PISTOL	40	TWO GROOMS
24	POINS	41	RUMOURS, *the Presenter*
25	PETO	42	A DANCER, *speaker of the*
26	SHALLOW		*Epilogue*
27	SILENCE *country justices*	43	LADY NORTHUMBERLAND
28	DAVY, *servant to Shallow*	44	LADY PERCY
29	MOULDY	45	MISTRESS QUICKLY, *hostess of a*
30	SHADOW		*tavern in Eastcheap*
31	WART *recruits*	46	DOLL TEARSHEET
32	FEEBLE		
33	BULLCALF	47	NON-SPEAKING: *Earl of Surrey,*
34	FANG		*Blunt, Lords, Beadles,*
35	SNARE *sheriff's officers*		*Musicians, and Attendants*
36	A PORTER		
37	TWO DRAWERS	48	SCENE: *England*

MUCH ADO ABOUT NOTHING

DRAMATIS PERSONÆ

1	DON PEDRO, *Prince of Arragon*	12	VERGES, *a headborough*
2	DON JOHN, *his bastard brother*	13	A SEXTON
3	CLAUDIO, *a young lord of*	14	A BOY
	Florence	15	TWO MESSENGERS
4	BENEDICK, *a young lord of*	16	TWO WATCHMEN
	Padua	17	A LORD
5	LEONATO, *Governor of Messina*	18	HERO, *daughter to Leonato*
6	ANTONIO, *his brother*	19	BEATRICE, *niece to Leonato*
7	BALTHASAR, *attendant on Don*	20	MARGARET *gentlewomen*
	Pedro	21	URSULA *attending on Hero*
8	CONRADE *followers of*	22	NON-SPEAKING: *Messengers,*
9	BORACHIO *Don John*		*Watch, Attendants, and*
10	FRIAR FRANCIS		*Musicians*
11	DOGBERRY, *a constable*		

The Life of
KING HENRY THE FIFTH

DRAMATIS PERSONÆ

1	KING HENRY THE FIFTH	26	A HERALD
2	DUKE OF	27	THREE MESSENGERS
	GLOUCESTER *brothers*	28	CHARLES THE SIXTH, *King of*
3	DUKE OF *to the King*		*France*
	BEDFORD	29	LEWIS, THE DAUPHIN
4	DUKE OF EXETER, *Uncle to the*	30	DUKE OF BURGUNDY
	King	31	DUKE OF ORLEANS
5	DUKE OF YORK, *cousin to the*	32	DUKE OF BOURBON
	King	33	THE CONSTABLE OF FRANCE
6	EARL OF SALISBURY	34	RAMBURES
7	EARL OF WESTMORELAND	35	GRANDPRÉ *French Lords*
8	EARL OF WARWICK	36	GOVERNOR OF HARFLEUR
9	ARCHBISHOP OF CANTERBURY	37	MONTJOY, *a French Herald*
10	BISHOP OF ELY	38	AMBASSADOR *to the King of*
11	EARL OF CAMBRIDGE		*England*
12	LORD SCROOP	39	FRENCH PRISONER
13	SIR THOMAS GREY	40	ISABEL, *Queen of France*
14	SIR THOMAS	41	KATHARINE, *daughter to Charles*
	ERPINGHAM		*and Isabel*
15	GOWER *officers in*	42	ALICE, *a lady attending on her*
16	FLUELLEN *King Henry's*	43	HOSTESS *of a tavern in*
17	MACMORRIS *army*		*Eastcheap, formerly* MISTRESS
18	JAMY		QUICKLY, *and now married to*
19	BATES		*Pistol*
20	COURT *soldiers in*	44	CHORUS
21	WILLIAMS *King Henry's army*	45	NON-SPEAKING: *Lords, Ladies,*
22	PISTOL		*Officers, Soldiers, Citizens,*
23	NYM		*and Attendants*
24	BARDOLPH		
25	BOY		

JULIUS CÆSAR

DRAMATIS PERSONÆ

1	JULIUS CÆSAR, *later as a* GHOST	5	CICERO
2	OCTAVIUS CÆSAR	6	PUBLIUS *Senators*
3	MARCUS ANTONIUS *Triumvirs*	7	POPILIUS LENA
4	M. ÆMILIUS *after the*	8	MARCUS BRUTUS
	LEPIDUS *death of*	9	CASSIUS
	Julius	10	CASCA
	Cæsar	11	TREBONIUS

12	LIGARIUS	*conspirators against Julius Cæsar*
13	DECIUS BRUTUS	
14	METELLUS CIMBER	
15	CINNA	
16	FLAVIUS	*Tribunes*
17	MARULLUS	
18	ARTEMIDORUS OF CNIDOS, *a teacher of rhetoric*	
19	A SOOTHSAYER	
20	CINNA, *a poet*	
21	ANOTHER POET	
22	LUCILIUS	
23	TITINIUS	*friends to Brutus and Cassius*
24	MESSALA	
25	YOUNG CATO	
26	VOLUMNIUS	
27	VARRO	
28	CLITUS	

29	CLAUDIUS	*servants to Brutus*
30	STRATO	
31	LUCIUS	
32	DARDANIUS	
33	PINDARUS, *servant to Cassius*	
34	TWO COMMONERS	
35	A SERVANT *to Cæsar*	
36	A SERVANT *to Antony*	
37	A SERVANT *to Octavius*	
38	FOUR CITIZENS	
39	THREE SOLDIERS	
40	A MESSENGER	
41	CALPURNIA, *wife to Cæsar*	
42	PORTIA, *wife to Brutus*	
43	NON-SPEAKING: *Senators, Citizens, Guards, Soldiers, and Attendants*	

AS YOU LIKE IT

DRAMATIS PERSONÆ

1	DUKE SENIOR, *living in banishment*
2	FREDERICK, *his brother, and usurper of his dominions*
3	AMIENS	*lords attending on the banished Duke*
4	JAQUES	
5	LE BEAU, *a courtier attending upon Frederick*
6	CHARLES, *wrestler to Frederick*
7	OLIVER	*sons of Sir Rowland de Boys*
8	JAQUES	
9	ORLANDO	
10	ADAM	*servants to Oliver*
11	DENNIS	
12	TOUCHSTONE, *a clown*
13	SIR OLIVER MARTEXT, *a vicar*
14	CORIN	*shepherds*
15	SILVIUS	

16	WILLIAM, *a country fellow, in love with Audrey*
17	THREE LORDS, *attending on the banished Duke*
18	TWO LORDS, *attending on Frederick*
19	TWO PAGES, *attending on the banished Duke*
20	HYMEN
21	A FORESTER
22	ROSALIND, *daughter to the banished Duke*
23	CELIA, *daughter to Frederick*
24	PHEBE, *a shepherdess*
25	AUDREY, *a country wench*
26	NON-SPEAKING: *Lords, Foresters, and Attendants*

HAMLET
Prince of Denmark

DRAMATIS PERSONÆ

1 CLAUDIUS, *King of Denmark*
2 HAMLET, *son to the late, and nephew to the present, King*
3 POLONIUS, *Lord Chamberlain*
4 HORATIO, *friend to Hamlet*
5 LAERTES, *son to Polonius*
6 VOLTIMAND
7 CORNELIUS
8 ROSENCRANTZ
9 GUILDENSTERN *Courtiers*
10 OSRIC
11 A GENTLEMAN
12 A PRIEST
13 MARCELLUS
14 BERNARDO *Officers*
15 FRANCISCO, *a soldier*
16 REYNALDO, *servant to Polonius*

17 FIVE PLAYERS
18 TWO CLOWNS, *gravediggers*
19 FORTINBRAS, *Prince of Norway*
20 A CAPTAIN
21 ENGLISH AMBASSADORS
22 A LORD
23 A SOLDIER
24 TWO MESSENGERS
25 A SERVANT *to Horatio*
26 DANES
27 GHOST *of Hamlet's father*
28 GERTRUDE, *Queen of Denmark, and mother to Hamlet*
29 OPHELIA, *daughter to Polonius*
30 NON-SPEAKING: *Lords, Ladies, Officers, Soldiers, Sailors, and other Attendants*

THE MERRY WIVES OF WINDSOR

DRAMATIS PERSONÆ

1 SIR JOHN FALSTAFF
2 FENTON, *a gentleman*
3 SHALLOW, *a country justice*
4 SLENDER, *cousin to Shallow*
5 FORD *two gentlemen dwelling at*
6 PAGE *Windsor*
7 WILLIAM PAGE, *a boy, son to Page*
8 SIR HUGH EVANS, *a Welsh parson*
9 DOCTOR CAIUS, *a French physician*
10 HOST *of the Garter Inn*
11 BARDOLPH
12 PISTOL *sharpers attending on Falstaff*
13 NYM

14 ROBIN, *page to Falstaff*
15 SIMPLE, *servant to Slender*
16 JOHN RUGBY, *servant to Doctor Caius*
17 TWO SERVANTS *to Ford*
18 MISTRESS FORD
19 MISTRESS PAGE
20 ANNE PAGE, *her daughter*
21 MISTRESS QUICKLY, *servant to Doctor Caius*
22 SOME CHILDREN, *as fairies*
23 NON-SPEAKING: *Servants to Page and Ford*

TWELFTH NIGHT
Or, What You Will

DRAMATIS PERSONÆ

1 ORSINO, DUKE OF ILLYRIA
2 SEBASTIAN, *brother to Viola*
3 ANTONIO, *a sea captain, friend to Sebastian*
4 A SEA CAPTAIN, *friend to Viola*
5 VALENTINE *gentlemen attending*
6 CURIO *on the Duke*
7 SIR TOBY BELCH, *uncle to Olivia*
8 SIR ANDREW AGUECHEEK
9 MALVOLIO, *steward to Olivia*
10 FABIAN *servants to*
11 FESTE, A CLOWN *Olivia*

12 TWO OFFICERS
13 A PRIEST
14 A SERVANT *to Olivia*
15 OLIVIA
16 VIOLA
17 MARIA, *Olivia's woman*
18 NON-SPEAKING: *Lords, Sailors, Officers, Musicians, and other Attendants*

TROILUS AND CRESSIDA

DRAMATIS PERSONÆ

1 PRIAM, *King of Troy*
2 HECTOR
3 TROILUS
4 PARIS *his sons*
5 DEIPHOBUS
6 HELENUS
7 MARGARELON, *a bastard son of Priam*
8 ÆNEAS *Trojan commanders*
9 ANTENOR
10 CALCHAS, *a Trojan priest, taking part with the Greeks*
11 PANDARUS, *uncle to Cressida*
12 AGAMEMNON, *the Grecian general*
13 MENELAUS, *his brother*
14 ACHILLES
15 AJAX
16 ULYSSES *Grecian*
17 NESTOR *commanders*
18 DIOMEDES
19 PATROCLUS

20 THERSITES, *a deformed and scurrilous Grecian*
21 ALEXANDER, *servant to Cressida*
22 A BOY, *servant to Troilus*
23 A SERVANT *to Paris*
24 A SERVANT *to Diomedes*
25 A MYRMIDON
26 HELEN, *wife to Menelaus*
27 ANDROMACHE, *wife to Hector*
28 CASSANDRA, *daughter to Priam, a prophetess*
29 CRESSIDA, *daughter to Calchas*
30 NON-SPEAKING: *Trojan and Greek soldiers, Myrmidons, and Attendants*

ALL'S WELL THAT ENDS WELL

DRAMATIS PERSONÆ

1 KING OF FRANCE
2 DUKE OF FLORENCE
3 BERTRAM, *Count of Rousillon*
4 LAFEU, *an old lord*
5 PAROLLES, *a follower of Bertram*
6 TWO FRENCH LORDS *in the Florentine service*
7 RINALDO, *steward to the Countess*
8 A CLOWN, *servant to the Countess*
9 THREE FRENCH LORDS, *attending on the King*
10 A GENTLEMAN, *a stranger*
11 TWO SOLDIERS
12 A MESSENGER
13 COUNTESS OF ROUSILLON, *mother to Bertram*

14 HELENA, *a gentlewoman protected by the Countess*
15 A WIDOW *of Florence*
16 DIANA, *daughter to the Widow*
17 MARIANA, *neighbour and friend to the Widow*
18 NON-SPEAKING: *Lords, Officers; Soldiers, French and Florentine; Violenta, neighbour and friend to the Widow; Attendants*

MEASURE FOR MEASURE

DRAMATIS PERSONÆ

1 VINCENTIO, *the Duke*
2 ANGELO, *the Deputy*
3 ESCALUS, *an ancient Lord*
4 CLAUDIO, *a young gentleman*
5 LUCIO, *a fantastic*
6 TWO GENTLEMEN
7 PROVOST
8 THOMAS
9 PETER *two friars*
10 A JUSTICE
11 VARRIUS
12 ELBOW, *a simple constable*
13 FROTH, *a foolish gentleman*
14 POMPEY, *servant to Mistress Overdone*

15 ABHORSON, *an executioner*
16 BARNARDINE, *a dissolute prisoner*
17 A BOY
18 A MESSENGER
19 A SERVANT *to Angelo*
20 ISABELLA, *sister to Claudio*
21 MARIANA, *betrothed to Angelo*
22 JULIET, *beloved of Claudio*
23 FRANCISCA, *a nun*
24 MISTRESS OVERDONE, *a bawd*
25 NON-SPEAKING: *Lords, Officers, Citizens, and Attendants*

OTHELLO, the Moor of Venice

DRAMATIS PERSONÆ

1 DUKE OF VENICE
2 BRABANTIO, *a Senator*
3 TWO SENATORS
4 GRATIANO, *brother to Brabantio*
5 LODOVICO, *kinsman to Brabantio*
6 OTHELLO, a noble Moor in the service of the Venetian state
7 CASSIO, *his lieutenant*
8 IAGO, *his ancient*
9 RODERIGO, *a Venetian gentleman*
10 MONTANO, *Othello's predecessor in the government of Cyprus*
11 CLOWN, *servant to Othello*
12 TWO GENTLEMEN, *of Venice*
13 FOUR GENTLEMEN, *of Cyprus*
14 AN OFFICER
15 A HERALD
16 A MESSENGER
17 A SAILOR
18 A MUSICIAN
19 DESDEMONA, *daughter to Brabantio and wife to Othello*
20 EMILIA, *wife to Iago*
21 BIANCA, *mistress to Cassio*
22 NON-SPEAKING: *Officers, Gentlemen, Musicians, and Attendants*

KING LEAR

DRAMATIS PERSONÆ

1 LEAR, *King of Britain*
2 KING OF FRANCE
3 DUKE OF BURGUNDY
4 DUKE OF CORNWALL
5 DUKE OF ALBANY
6 EARL OF KENT
7 EARL OF GLOUCESTER
8 EDGAR, *son to Gloucester*
9 EDMUND, *bastard son to Gloucester*
10 CURAN, *a courtier*
11 OLD MAN, *tenant to Gloucester*
12 A DOCTOR
13 FOOL
14 OSWALD, *steward to Goneril*
15 TWO CAPTAINS
16 A GENTLEMAN, *attendant on Cordelia*
17 A GENTLEMAN, *attendant on Lear*
18 A KNIGHT, *attendant on Lear*
19 A HERALD
20 THREE SERVANTS *to Cornwall*
21 TWO MESSENGERS
22 GONERIL
23 REGAN   *daughters to Lear*
24 CORDELIA
25 NON-SPEAKING: *Knights of Lear's train, Captains, Soldiers, and Attendants*

MACBETH

DRAMATIS PERSONÆ

1 DUNCAN, *King of Scotland*
2 MALCOLM   *his sons*
3 DONALBAIN
4 MACBETH *generals of the*
5 BANQUO *King's army*
6 MACDUFF

7	LENNOX		21	AN OLD MAN
8	ROSS	noblemen of	22	A SERGEANT
9	MENTEITH	Scotland	23	TWO MESSENGERS
10	ANGUS		24	AN ATTENDANT on Macbeth
11	CAITHNESS		25	A SERVANT to Lady Macbeth
12	FLEANCE, son to Banquo		26	THREE MURDERERS
13	SIWARD, Earl of Northumberland, general of the English forces		27	LADY MACBETH
			28	LADY MACDUFF
			29	A GENTLEWOMAN, attending on Lady Macbeth
14	YOUNG SIWARD, his son			
15	SEYTON, an officer attending on Macbeth		30	HECATE
			31	THREE WITCHES
16	BOY, son to Macduff		32	THREE APPARITIONS
17	AN ENGLISH DOCTOR		33	NON-SPEAKING: Lords, Ladies, Officers, Soldiers, Ghosts, and Attendants
18	A SCOTCH DOCTOR			
19	A LORD			
20	A PORTER			

ANTONY AND CLEOPATRA

DRAMATIS PERSONÆ

1	MARK ANTONY		24	EUPHRONIUS, an ambassador from Antony to Cæsar
2	OCTAVIUS CÆSAR	triumvirs		
3	M. ÆMILIUS LEPIDUS		25	ALEXAS
4	SEXTUS POMPEIUS		26	MARDIAN, a eunuch attendants on Cleopatra
5	DOMITIUS ENOBARBUS		27	SELEUCUS
6	VENTIDIUS		28	DIOMEDES
7	EROS	friends to Antony	29	A SOOTHSAYER
8	SCARUS		30	A CLOWN
9	DERCETAS		31	FIVE MESSENGERS
10	DEMETRIUS		32	AN EGYPTIAN
11	PHILO		33	TWO SERVANTS to Pompey
12	MECÆNAS		34	A CAPTAIN of Antony's army
13	AGRIPPA		35	FOUR SOLDIERS of Antony's army
14	DOLABELLA	friends to Cæsar	36	FOUR SOLDIERS of Cæsar's army
15	PROCULEIUS		37	TWO GUARDS to Cleopatra
16	THYREUS		38	THREE GUARDS of Antony's army
17	GALLUS		39	TWO ATTENDANTS on Antony
18	MENAS		40	ONE ATTENDANT on Cleopatra
19	MENECRATES	friends to Pompey	41	CLEOPATRA, Queen of Egypt
20	VARRIUS		42	OCTAVIA, sister to Cæsar and wife to Antony
21	TAURUS, lieutenant-general to Cæsar		43	CHARMIAN attendants on
22	CANIDIUS, lieutenant-general to Antony		44	IRAS Cleopatra
23	SILIUS, an officer in Ventidius' army		45	NON-SPEAKING: Officers, Soldiers, Guards, Servitors, and Attendants

CORIOLANUS

DRAMATIS PERSONÆ

1 CAIUS MARCIUS, *afterwards*
   CAIUS MARCIUS CORIOLANUS
2 TITUS LARTIUS   *generals against*
3 COMINIUS   *the Volscians*
4 MENENIUS AGRIPPA, *friend to*
   Coriolanus
5 SICINIUS VELUTUS   *tribunes of*
6 JUNIUS BRUTUS   *the people*
7 YOUNG MARCIUS, *son to*
   Coriolanus
8 A ROMAN HERALD
9 NICANOR, *a Roman*
10 AN ÆDILE
11 TWO PATRICIANS
12 TWO OFFICERS
13 A LIEUTENANT *to Lartius*
14 TWO SENATORS
15 SEVEN CITIZENS
16 THREE MESSENGERS
17 THREE SOLDIERS
18 TULLUS AUFIDIUS, *general of the*
   Volscians

19 A LIEUTENANT *to Aufidius*
20 THREE CONSPIRATORS *with*
   Aufidius
21 A CITIZEN *of Antium*
22 TWO LORDS
23 TWO SENTRIES
24 TWO SENATORS
25 THREE SOLDIERS
26 ADRIAN, *A Volscian*
27 THREE SERVANTS *to Aufidius*
28 VOLUMNIA, *mother to Coriolanus*
29 VIRGILIA, *wife to Coriolanus*
30 VALERIA, *friend to Virgilia*
31 GENTLEWOMAN, *attending on*
   Virgilia
32 NON-SPEAKING: *Roman and*
   Volscian Senators, Patricians,
   Soldiers, Citizens, Lictors, and
   Attendants

TIMON OF ATHENS

DRAMATIS PERSONÆ

1 TIMON *of Athens*
2 LUCIUS
3 LUCULLUS   *flattering lords*
4 SEMPRONIUS
5 VENTIDIUS, *one of Timon's false*
   friends
6 ALCIBIADES, *an Athenian captain*
7 APEMANTUS, *a churlish*
   philosopher
8 FLAVIUS, *steward to Timon*
9 A POET
10 A PAINTER
11 A JEWELLER
12 A MERCHANT
13 AN OLD ATHENIAN
14 A PAGE
15 A FOOL

16 THREE STRANGERS
17 A SOLDIER
18 THREE BANDITTI
19 FOUR SENATORS
20 FOUR LORDS
21 THREE MESSENGERS
22 FLAMINIUS
23 LUCILIUS   *Servants to Timon*
24 SERVILIUS
25 CAPHIS
26 PHILOTUS   *Servants to*
27 TITUS   *Timon's creditors*
28 HORTENSIUS
29 THREE SERVANTS *to Timon*
30 TWO SERVANTS *to Varro*
31 A SERVANT *to Isidore*
32 A SERVANT *to Lucullus*

33 A SERVANT *to Lucius*
34 PHRYNIA   *mistresses to*
35 TIMANDRA   *Alcibiades*
36 CUPID

37 AMAZONS   *in the mask*
38 NON-SPEAKING: *Lords, Senators,*
      Officers, Soldiers, Banditti,
      and Attendants

PERICLES
Prince of Tyre

DRAMATIS PERSONÆ

1   GOWER, *as Chorus*
2   ANTIOCHUS, *King of Antioch*
3   PERICLES, *Prince of Tyre*
4   HELICANUS   *two lords of Tyre*
5   ESCANES
6   SIMONIDES, *King of Pentapolis*
7   CLEON, *governor of Tarsus*
8   LYSIMACHUS, *governor of*
      Mytilene
9   CERIMON, *a lord of Ephesus*
10 THALIARD, *a lord of Antioch*
11 PHILEMON, *servant to Cerimon*
12 LEONINE, *servant to Dionyza*
13 MARSHAL
14 A PANDAR
15 BOULT, *his servant*
16 A MESSENGER
17 THREE LORDS *of Tyre*
18 A LORD *of Tarsus*
19 THREE FISHERMEN
20 A KNIGHT, *attending on*
      Simonides

21 TWO SAILORS *of Pentapolis*
22 A SERVANT *to Cerimon*
23 THREE PIRATES
24 TWO GENTLEMEN *of Mytilene*
25 A SAILOR *of Tyre*
26 A SAILOR *of Mytilene*
27 FIVE KNIGHTS, *suitors to Thaisa*
28 THE DAUGHTER *of Antiochus*
29 DIONYZA, *wife to Cleon*
30 THAISA, *daughter to Simonides*
31 MARINA, *daughter to Pericles and*
      Thaisa
32 LYCHORIDA, *nurse to Marina*
33 A BAWD
34 DIANA
35 NON-SPEAKING: *Lords, Knights,*
      Gentlemen, Sailors, and
      Attendants

CYMBELINE

DRAMATIS PERSONÆ

1   CYMBELINE, *King of Britain*
2   CLOTEN, *son to the Queen by a*
      former husband
3   POSTHUMUS LEONATUS, *a*
      gentleman, husband to Imogen
4   BELARIUS, *a banished lord,*
      disguised under the name of
      Morgan
5   GUIDERIUS   *sons to Cymbeline,*

6   ARVIRAGUS *disguised under the*
      names of Polydore
      and Cadwal, sup-
      posed sons to
      Morgan
7   PHILARIO,
      friend to Posthumus
                        Italians
8   IACHIMO,
      friend to Philario

9	CAIUS LUCIUS, *general of the Roman forces*	25	QUEEN, *wife to Cymbeline*
10	PISANIO, *servant to Posthumus*	26	IMOGEN, *daughter to Cymbeline by a former Queen*
11	CORNELIUS, *a physician*	27	HELEN, *a lady attending on Imogen*
12	A ROMAN CAPTAIN		
13	TWO BRITISH CAPTAINS	28	A LADY *attending on the Queen*
14	A FRENCHMAN	29	SICILIUS LEONATUS, *father to Posthumus*
15	A SPANIARD	*friends to Philario*		
16	A DUTCHMAN	30	TWO LEONATI, *brothers to Posthumus* Apparitions
17	TWO LORDS *of Cymbeline's court*		
18	TWO GENTLEMEN *of Cymbeline's court*	31	MOTHER *to Posthumus*
19	TWO GAOLERS	32	JUPITER
20	A SOOTHSAYER	33	NON-SPEAKING: *Lords, Ladies, Roman Senators and Tribunes, Musicians, Officers, Captains, Soldiers, and Attendants*
21	A TRIBUNE		
22	TWO SENATORS		
23	AN ATTENDANT *on Cymbeline*		
24	TWO MESSENGERS		

THE WINTER'S TALE

DRAMATIS PERSONÆ

1	TIME, *as Chorus*	17	A LORD, *attending on Leontes*
2	LEONTES, *King of Sicilia*	18	THREE SERVANTS *to Leontes*
3	MAMILLIUS, *young Prince of Sicilia*	19	AN OFFICER
		20	A SERVANT *to the Old Shepherd*
4	CAMILLO	21	HERMIONE, *Queen to Leontes*
5	ANTIGONUS	*four Lords of*	22	PERDITA, *daughter to Leontes and Hermione*
6	CLEOMENES	*Sicilia*		
7	DION	23	PAULINA, *wife to Antigonus*
8	POLIXENES, *King of Bohemia*	24	EMILIA, *a lady attending on Hermione*
9	FLORIZEL, *Prince of Bohemia*		
10	ARCHIDAMUS, *a Lord of Bohemia*	25	MOPSA	*shepherdesses*
11	OLD SHEPHERD, *reputed father of Perdita*	26	DORCAS	
		27	TWO LADIES *attending on Hermione*
12	CLOWN, *his son*		
13	AUTOLYCUS, *a rogue*	28	NON-SPEAKING: *Lords, Ladies, Gentlemen, Officers, Servants, Shepherds, Shepherdesses, and Attendants*
14	A MARINER		
15	A GAOLER		
16	THREE GENTLEMEN		

THE TEMPEST

DRAMATIS PERSONÆ

1	ALONSO, *King of Naples*	4	ANTONIO, *his brother, the usurping Duke of Milan*
2	SEBASTIAN, *his brother*		
3	PROSPERO, *the right Duke of Milan*	5	FERDINAND, *son to the King of Naples*

6	GONZALO, *an honest old counsellor*	14	MARINERS
7	ADRIAN	15	MIRANDA, *daughter to Prospero*
8	FRANCISCO	*Lords*	16	ARIEL, *an airy spirit*
9	CALIBAN, *a savage and deformed slave*	17	IRIS
10	TRINCULO, *a jester*	18	CERES	*Spirits*
11	STEPHANO, *a drunken butler*	19	JUNO
12	MASTER *of a ship*	20	NON-SPEAKING: *Nymphs and Reapers, presented by Spirits; and other Spirits attending on Prospero*
13	BOATSWAIN		

The Famous History of the Life of
KING HENRY THE EIGHTH

DRAMATIS PERSONÆ

1 KING HENRY THE EIGHTH
2 CARDINAL WOLSEY
3 CARDINAL CAMPEIUS
4 CAPUCIUS, *ambassador from the Emperor Charles V*
5 CRANMER, *Archbishop of Canterbury*
6 DUKE OF NORFOLK
7 DUKE OF BUCKINGHAM
8 DUKE OF SUFFOLK
9 EARL OF SURREY
10 LORD CHAMBERLAIN
11 LORD CHANCELLOR
12 GARDINER, *Bishop of Winchester*
13 BISHOP OF LINCOLN
14 LORD ABERGAVENNY
15 LORD SANDS
16 SIR HENRY GUILDFORD
17 SIR THOMAS LOVELL
18 SIR ANTHONY DENNY
19 SIR NICHOLAS VAUX
20 TWO SECRETARIES *to Wolsey*
21 CROMWELL, *servant to Wolsey*
22 GRIFFITH, *gentleman-usher to Queen Katharine*
23 THREE GENTLEMEN
24 DOCTOR BUTTS, *physician to the King*
25 GARTER KING-AT-ARMS

26 SURVEYOR *to the Duke of Buckingham*
27 BRANDON
28 SERGEANT-AT-ARMS
29 DOOR-KEEPER *of the Council-chamber*
30 PORTER
31 MAN, *to the Porter*
32 PAGE *to Gardiner*
33 A CRIER
34 A MESSENGER
35 A SCRIBE
36 A SERVANT *to Wolsey*
37 QUEEN KATHARINE, *wife to King Henry, afterwards divorced*
38 ANNE BULLEN, *her Maid of Honour, afterwards Queen*
39 AN OLD LADY, *friend to Anne Bullen*
40 PATIENCE, *woman to Queen Katharine*
41 NON-SPEAKING: *Lords and Ladies in the Dumb Shows, Women attending on the Queen, Scribes, Officers, Guards, Attendants, and Six Spirits appearing to Queen Katharine*

CHAPTER EIGHT

VOCABULARY

Prefixes

Prefix	Meaning	Example
a-, an- (G)	without, not	amorphous
ab-, abs- (L)	away, from, apart	absent
ad-, ac-, af- (L)	to, towards	advent, advance
aero-	air	aeroplane, aeronaut
amb-, ambi- (G)	both, around	ambiguous
amphi- (G)	both, around	amphitheatre
ante- (L)	before	antenatal
anti- (G)	against	antidote, antitoxic
apo-	away from	apostasy
arch- (G)	chief, most important	archbishop, archcriminal
auto- (G)	self	automatic, autocrat
be-	about, make	belittle, beguile, beset
bene- (L)	well, good	benediction
bi- (G)	two	biennial, bicycle
by-, bye- (G)	added to	by ways, by-laws
cata- (G)	down	catalogue, cataract
centi-, cente- (L)	hundred	centigrade, centenary
circum- (L)	around	circumference, circumambient
co-, col-, com-, cor-	together	companion
con- (L)	with,	collect, co-operate
contra- (L)	against, counter	contradict, contraceptive
de- (F)	down	denude, decentralise
deca-, deci- (G)	ten	decade, decagon
demi- (L)	half	demigod
dia- (G)	through, between	diameter
dis- (L)	not, opposite to	dislike, disagree
duo- (G)	two	duologue, duplex
dys-	ill, hard	dysentery
e-, ex- (L)	out of	exhale, excavate
ec- (L)	out of	eccentric
en-, in-, em-, im-, (L; G) (F)	into, not	enrage, inability, embolden, emulate, impress
epi- (G)	upon, at, in addition	epidemic, epidermis

Prefix	Meaning	Example
equi-	equally	equidistant
extra- (L)	outside, beyond	extra-essential
for-, fore- (E)	before	foresee
hemi- (G)	half	hemisphere
hepta- (G)	seven	heptagon
hexa- (G)	six	hexagon, hexateuch
homo- (L)	same	homonym
hyper- (G)	above, excessive	hypercritical, hypertrophy
il-	not	illegal, illogical
in-, im- (un) (L, G, F)	not	imperfect, inaccessible
inter- (L)	among, between	interrupt, intermarriage
intra-, intro- (L)	inside, within	intramural, introvert
iso- (G)	equal, same	isobaric, isosceles
mal- (L)	bad, wrong	malfunction, malformed
meta- (G)	after, beyond	metabolism, metaphysical
mis-	wrongly	misfit, mislead
mono- (G)	one, single	monotonous, monocular
multi- (L)	many	multipurpose, multimillion
non-	not	nonsense, nonpareil
ob-, oc-, of-, op- (L)	in the way of, resistance	obstruct, obstacle, oppose
octa-, octo- (G)	eight	octahedron, octave
off-	away, apart	offset
out-	beyond	outnumber, outstanding
over-	above	overhear, overcharge
para- (G)	aside, beyond	parable, paradox
penta- (G)	five	pentagon, pentateuch
per- (L)	through	perennial, peradventure
peri- (G)	around, about	perimeter, pericardium
poly- (G)	many	polygamy, polytechnic
post- (L)	after	postscript, postnatal
pre- (L)	before	prehistoric, pre-war
prime-, primo- (L)	first, important	primary, Prime Minister
pro- (L)	in front of, favouring	prologue, pro-British
quadri- (L)	four	quadriennial, quadrangle
re- (L)	again, back	reappear, recivilise
retro- (L)	backward	retrograde, retrospect
se-	aside	secede
self-	personalising	selfcontrol, selftaught
semi- (G)	half	semicircle, semidetached
sub- (L)	under	submarine, subterranean
super- (L)	above, over	superfluous, superior
syl-	with, together	syllogism
syn-, sym- (G)	together	sympathy, synchronise
tele- (G)	far, at or to a distance	telegram, telepathy
ter- (L)	three times	tercentenary

Prefix	Meaning	Example
tetra- (G)	four	tetrahedron, tetralogy
trans- (L)	across, through	transatlantic, translate
tri- (L; G)	three	triangle, tripartite
ultra- (L)	beyond	ultramarine, ultra-violet
un- (im) (L, G, F)	not	unbroken, unbutton, unable
under-	below	underfed, underling
uni- (L)	one	unicellular, uniform
vice- (L)	in place of	viceroy, vice-president
yester- (E)	preceding time	yesterday, yesteryear

Suffixes

Suffix	Meaning	Example
-able, -ible (L)	capable of, fit for	durable, comprehensible
-acy (L; G)	state or quality of	accuracy
-age (L)	action or state of	breakage
-al, -ial (L)	relating to	abdominal
-an (ane, ian) (L)	the nature of	Grecian, African
-ance, ence	quality or action of	insurance, corpulence
-ant (L)	forming adjectives of quality, nouns signifying a personal agent or something producing an effect	defiant, servant
-arium, -orium (L)	place for	aquarium, auditorium
-ary (L)	place for, dealing with	seminary, dictionary
-atable (L)	See -able, -ible	
-ate (L)	cause to be, office of	animate, magistrate
-ation, -ition (L)	action or state of	condition, dilapidation
-cle, -icle (L)	diminutive	icicle
-dom (E)	condition or control	kingdom
-en (E)	small	mitten
-en (E)	quality	golden, broken
-er (E)	belonging to	farmer, New Yorker
-ess (E)	feminine suffix	hostess, waitress
-et, ette (L)	small	puppet, marionette
-ferous (L)	producing	coniferous
-ful (E)	full of	colourful, beautiful
-fy, ify (L)	make	satisfy, fortify
-hood (E)	state or condition of	boyhood, childhood
-ia (L)	names of classes, names of places	bacteria, America
-ian (L)	practioners or inhabitants	musician, Parisian
-ion (L)	condition or action of	persuasion
-ic (G)	relating to	historic

Suffix	Meaning	Example
-id(e) (L)	a quality	acid
-ine (G; L)	a compound	chlorine
-ish (E)	a similarity or relationship	childish, greenish
-ism (G)	quality or doctrine of	realism, socialism
-ist (G)	one who practices	chemist, pessimist
-itis (L)	inflammation of (medical)	bronchitis
-ity, -ety, ty (L)	state or quality of	loyalty
-ive (L)	nature of	creative, receptive
-ize, ise (G)	make, practise, act like	modernize, advertise
-lent (L)	fulness	violent
-less (E)	lacking	fearless, faceless
-logy (G)	indicating a branch of knowledge	biology, psychology
-ly (E)	having the quality of	softly, quickly
-ment (L)	act or condition of	resentment
-metry, -meter (G)	measurement	gasometer, geometry
-mony	resulting condition	testimony
-oid (G)	resembling	ovoid
-or (L)	a state or action, a person who, or thing which	error, governor, victor, generator
-osis	process or condition of	metamorphosis
-ous, -ose (L)	full of	murderous, anxious, officious, morose
-some	like	gladsome
-tude (L)	quality or degree of	attitude, gratitude
-ward (E)	direction	backward, outward
-y (E)	condition	difficulty

Roots

Root	Meaning	Example
aer	air	aerate, aeroplane
am (fr. amare)	love	amorous, amateur, amiable
ann (fr. annus)	year	annual, anniversary
aud, (fr. audire)	hear	auditorium, audit
bio	life	biography
cap (fr. capire)	take	captive
cap (fr. caput)	head	capital, per capita, decapitate
chron	time	chronology, chronic
cor	heart	cordial

Root	Meaning	Example
corp	body	corporation
de	god	deify, deity
dic, dict	say, speak	dictate
duc, (fr. ducere)	lead	aqueduct, duke, ductile
ego	I	egotism
equi	equal	equidistant
fac, fic, (fr. facere)	make, do	manufacture, efficient
frat	brother	fraternity
geo	earth	geology
graph	write	calligraphy, graphology, telegraph
loc (fr. locus)	place	location, local
loqu, loc (fr. loqui)	speak	eloquence, circumlocution
luc, (fr. lux)	light	elucidate
man (fr. manus)	hand	manuscript, manipulate
mit, miss (fr. mittere)	send	admit, permission
mort, (fr. mors)	death	immortal
omni	all	omnipotent, omnibus
pat (fr. pater)	father	paternal
path	suffering, feeling	sympathy, pathology
ped, (fr. pes)	foot	impede, millepede, pedal
phobia, phobe	fear	hydrophobe, xenophobia
photo	light	photography
pneum	air, breath, spirit	pneumonia
pos, posit	place	deposit, position
pot, poss, poten, (fr. ponerte)	be able	potential, possible
quaerere	ask, question, seek	inquiry, query
rog, (fr. rogare)	ask	interrogate
scrib, scrip, (fr. scribere)	write	scribble, script, inscribe
sent, sens, (fr. sentire)	feel	sensitive, sentiment
sol	alone	soloist, isolate
soph	wise	philosopher
spect, (fr. spicere)	look	introspective, inspect
spir, (fr. spirate)	breathe	inspiration
ten, (fr. tendere)	stretch	extend, tense
ten, (fr. tenere)	hold	tenant
therm, (fr. thermos)	warm	thermometer
utilis	useful	utility
ven, vent (fr. venire)	come, arrive	advent, convenient
vert, vers, (fr. vertere)	turn	revert, adverse
vid, vis (fr. videre)	see	supervisor, vision, provident

CHAPTER NINE

LANGUAGES

Fifty percent of all spoken language is composed of 100 basic key words. For this reason *Master Your Memory* has included the hundred basic words from ten of the world's most common languages.

Applying SEMMG to languages, you simply mark off one of the thousand cross grids, say 5000 to 5999, and apply the Memory Principles as before.

For example, if you were going to visit Italy, and wished to learn the first 100 words of the Italian vocabulary, and were using the Sensation 1000 Memory Grid, and were wanting to remember the third word in the list 'tutto', which means 'all', you would take the Key Memory Image 5003 your mother swimming in an Italian sea or lake. You would *feel* the sensation that your mother felt as she swam, and looked around, taking in *ALL* that was moving and going on around her, as you envisioned her feeling her *TWO TOES* at the same time!

Memorising vocabulary in this way not only helps you memorise the vocabulary, but helps you also use imagery and sensation, which recent research has discovered are major elements in any successful language learning.

5000   Swimming

English	Italian	Italian Pronunciation
0 After	Dietro	Dee-ay'troh
1 Again Dew	Di nuovo	Dee-noo-oh'voh
2 All new	Tutto	Toot'toh
3 Almost Ma	Quasi	Kwah'zee
4 Also Rah	Anche	Ahng'kay
5 Although Law	Sebbene	Seb-bay'nay
6 Always Jaw	Sempre	Sem'pray
7 And Keys	E	Ay
8 A, an Fee	Un, una	Oon, oona

103

English	Italian	Italian Pronunciation
Because	Perche	Pehr'kay
Before	Davanti	Dah-vahn'tee
Big	Grande	Grahn'day
But	Ma	Mah
Can (I can)	Io posso	Ee'oh poss-oh
Come (I come)	Io vengo	Ee'oh ven'go
Either/or	O/o	Oh/oh
Find (I find)	Io trovo	Ee'oh troh-voh
First	Primo	Pree-moh
For	Per	Pehr
Friend	Amico	Am-ee'coh
From	Da	Dah
Good	Buono	Boo-oh'noh
Goodbye	Ciao	Chow
Happy	Selice	Se'lee'cheh
Have (I have)	Io ho	Ee'oh ho
He	Lui	Loo'ee
Hello	Buongiorno	Boo'on-jorr'noh
Here	Qui	Kwee
I	Io	Ee'oh
I am	Sono	Soh'noh
If	Se	Say
In	In	Een
Know (I know)	Io conosco	Ee'oh koh-noh-sho
Last	Scorso	Skorr'soh
Like (I like)	Io piaccio	Ee'oh pee-ah-cho
Little	Poco	Poh'koh
Love (I love)	Io amo	Eeh'oh am'oh
Many	Molti	Moll-tee
Me	Mi	May
More	Piu	Pee'oo
Most	Il piu	Eel pee'oo
Mr	Signore	Seen-yoh'ray
Much	Molto	Moll'toh
My	Mio	Mee'oh
Never	Mai	Mah'ee
New	Nuovo	Noo-oh'voh
Next	Prossimo	Pross'see-moh
No	No	Noh
Not	Non	Nonn
Now	Ora	Oh'rah
Of	Di	Dee
Often	Spesso	Spess'soh

English	Italian	Italian Pronunciation
Old	Vecchio	Veck'kee-oh
On	Su	Soo
One	Uno	Oon'oh
Only	Solo	Soh'loh
Or	O	Oh
Other	Altro	Ahl'troh
Our	Il nostro	Eel noss'troh
Out	Fuori	Foo-oh'ree
Over	Attraverso	Aht'trah-vehr'soh
Part	Parte	Pahr'tay
People	Gente	Jen'tay
Place	Luogo	Loo-oh'goh
Please	Per favore	Pehr fah-voh'ray
Same	Medesimo	May-day'zeemoh
See (I see)	Io vedo	Eeh'oh vay-doh
She	Lei	Lay'ee
So	Cosi	Koh'see
Some	Qualche	Kwahl'kay
Sometimes	Talvolta	Tahl-voll'tah
Still	Ancora	Ahng'koh-rah
Such	Tale	Tah'lay
Than	Di	Dee
Thank you	Grazie	Grah'tsee
That	Quello	Kwell'loh
The	Il, la	Eel, lah
Their	Il loro, la loro	Eel loh'roh, lah loh'roh
Them	Li, le, loro	Lee, lay, loh'roh
Then	Allora	Ahl-loh'rah
There is, There are	C'e, ci sono	Chay, chee soh-noh
They	Loro	Loh'roh
Thing	Cosa	Koh'sah
Think (I think)	Io penso	Eeh'oh pen-soh
This	Questo	Kwess'toh
Through	Diretto	Dee-ret'toh
Time	Ora	Oh'rah
To	Per	Pehr
Under	Piu basso	Pee-oo bahs'soh
Up	Su per	Soo pehr
Us	Noi	Noh'ee
Use (I use)	Io uso	Eeh'oh oo-zoh
Very	Molto	Moll'toh
We	Noi	Noh'ee

English	Italian	Italian Pronunciation
What	Come	Koh'may
When	Quando	Kwahn'doh
Where	Dove	Doh'vay
With	Con	Kon
Yes	Si	See
You	Tu	Too
Your	Il suo, la sua	Eel soo'oh, lah soo'ah

English	French	French Pronunciation
After	Apres	A'pray
Again	Encore	O(n)'kor
All	Tout, toute	Too, toot
Almost	Presque	Press'ke
Also	Aussi	Oh'see
Although	Bien que	Bee'a(n)'ke
Always	Toujours	Too'shure
And	Et	Ay
A, an	Un, une	Er(n), oon
Because	Parce que	Pah'ske
Before	Avant	A'vo(n)
Big	Grand	Gro(n)
But	Mais	May
Can (I can)	Je peux	★Je pe
Come (I come)	Je viens	★Je vee'a(n)
Either/or	Ou/ou	Ooh/ooh
Find (I find)	Je trouve	★Je troov
First	Premier	Preh'mee'ay
For	Pour	Poor
Friend	Ami	Am'ee
From	De	De
Good	Bien	Bee'a(n)
Goodbye	Au revoir	O-re'vwa
Happy	Content	Ko(n)'to(n)
Have (I have)	J'ai	★Jay
He	Il	Eel
Hello	Bonjour	Bo(n)'shure
Here	Ici	Ee'see
I	Je	★Je
I am	Je suis	★Je swee
If	Si	See

106

English	French	French Pronunciation
In	Dans	Do(n)
Know (I know)	Je sais	*Je say
Last	Dernier	Dair'nee'ay
Like (I like)	J'aime	*Jem
Little	Petit	Pe'tee
Love (I love)	J'aime	*Jem
Many	Beaucoup	Bo'ku
Me	Moi	Mwa
More	Plus	Ploo
Most	La plupart	La ploo'par
Mr	Monsieur	Mo(n)'s'ure
Much	Beaucoup	Bo'ku
My	Mon	Mo(n)
Never	Jamais	*Ja'may
New	Nouveau, nouvelle	Nu'vo, nu'vel
Next	Prochain	Prosh'a(n)
No	Non	No(n)
Not	Ne pas	Ne pah
Now	Maintenant	Ma(n)'te'no(n)
Of	De	De
Often	Souvent	Soo'vo(n)
Old	Vieux	Vje
On	Sur	S'ure
One	Un	Er(n)
Only	Seulement	Serl'e'mo(n)
Or	Ou	Ooh
Other	Autre	Oh'tr
Our	Notre	No'tr
Out	Dehors	De'or
Over	Pardessus	Par'de'soo
Part	Partie	Pah'tee
People	Les gens	Lay *jo(n)
Place	Place	Plas
Please	S'il vous plait	See voo play
Same	Meme	Memm
See (I see)	Je vois	*Je vwa
She	Elle	El
So	Donc	Do(n)k
Some	Quelque	Kel'ke
Sometimes	Quelquefois	Kel'ke fwa
Still	Encore	O(n)'kor
Such	Tel	Tell
Than	Que	Ke

English	French	French Pronunciation
Thank you	Merci	Mair'see
That	Que	Ke
The	Le, la	Le, lah
Their	Leur	Ler
Them	Les	Lay
Then	Alors	Ahl-loh're
There is, There are	Il y a	Eel ee ar
They	Ils, elles	Eel, ell
Thing	Chose	Sh'ohs
Think (I think)	Je pense	*Je po(n)se
This	Ce, cette	Se, set
Through	A travers	Ah tra'vair
Time	Temps	To(n)
To	A	Ah
Under	Sous	Soo
Up	En haut	On'oh
Us	Nous	Noo
Use (I use)	J'utilise	*Joo'tee'lees
Very	Tres	Tray
We	Nous	Noo
What	Que	Ke
When	Quand	Ko(n)
Where	Ou	Ooh
With	Avec	A'vek
Yes	Oui	Wee
You	Tu, vous	Too, voo
Your	Ton, tes, votre, vos	To(n), tay, vot're, voh

NOTES:
French pronunciation: *Je is pronounced like (plea)sure or (bei)ge; where n is in brackets (n) pronounced nasally.

English	German	German Pronunciation
After	Nach	Nahk
Again	Wieder	Vee-dair
All	Alle	Ul-le
Almost	Beinahe	By-nah
Also	Auch	Owk
Although	Obgleich	Ob'gly'k

English	German	German Pronunciation
Always	Immer	Im'me
And	Und	Oont
A, an	Ein, eine	Ine, i-ne
Because	Weil	Vile
Before	Vorn	Fawn
Big	Gross	Grohs
But	Aber	Arb'e
Can (I can)	Ich kann	Ik kan
Come (I come)	Ich komme	Ik komm'e
Either/or	Entweder/oder	Ent'vay'de/oh'de
Find (I find)	Ich finde	Ik fin'de
First	Erst	Air'st
For	Fur	Fewr
Friend	Freund	Froynt
From	Von	Fon
Good	Gut	Goot
Goodbye	Auf wiedersehen	Owf'vee'dair-zay-en
Happy	Froh	Fro
Have (I have)	Ich habe	Ik hah'be
He	Er	Air
Hello	Guten tag	Goot'en tahg
Here	Hier	Heer
I	Ich	Ik
I am	Ich bin	Ik bin
If	Wenn	Ven
In	In	In
Know (I know)	Ich weiss	Ik vice
Last	Letzt	Let's't
Like (I like)	Ich liebe	Ik lee'be
Little	Klein	Kline
Love (I love)	Ich liebe	Ik lee'be
Many	Viel	Feel
Me	Mich	Mik
More	Mehr	M'air
Most	Die meisten	Dee my'sten
Mr	Herr	Hair
Much	Viel	Feel
My	Mein	Mine
Never	Nie	Nee
New	Neu	Noy
Next	Nachst	Next
No	Nein	Nine
Not	Nicht	Nikt

English	German	German Pronunciation
Now	Jetzt	Yet's't
Of	Von	Fon
Often	Oft	Off't
Old	Alt	Ult
On	Auf	Owf
One	Ein	Ine
Only	Nur	Newr
Or	Oder	O'de
Other	Andere	Un'de're
Our	Unser	Oon'sair
Out	Aus	Ows
Over	Uber	Oo'bair
Part	Der teil	Dair tile
People	Leute	Loy'te
Place	Platz	Plahts
Please	Bitte	Bitter
Same	Derselbe, dieselbe, dasselbe	Dair'sel'be, dee'sel'be, duss'sel'be
See (I see)	Ich sehe	Ik say'e
She	Sie	Zee
So	So	Zoh
Some	Etwas	Et'vahss
Sometimes	Manchmal	Monk'mahl
Still	Noch	Nok
Such	Solch	Solk
Than	Als	Uls
Thank you	Danke	Dahnn'ke
That	Das	Duss
The	Der, die, das	Dair, dee, duss
Their	Ihr	Eer
Them	Sie	Zee
Then	Dann	Dahnn
There is, There are	Es gibt	Ess gib't
They	Sie	Zee
Thing	Die sache	Dee sah'ke
Think (I think)	Ich denke	Ik den'ke
This	Diese	Dee'ze
Through	Durch	Doohrk
Time	Zeit	Tsite
To	Nach	Nahk
Under	Unter	Oon'te
Up	Auf	Ow'f

110

English	German	German Pronunciation
Us	Uns	Oon's
Use (I use)	Ich gebrauche	Ik gay'brow'ke
Very	Sehr	Zare
We	Wir	Veer
What	Wass	Vahss
When	Wann	Vun
Where	Wo	Voh
With	Mit	Mitt
Yes	Ja	Yah
You	Du, sie	Doo, zee
Your	Ihr, Euer	Eer, oy'e

English	Portuguese	Portuguese Pronunciation
After	Depois	De-poh'eesh
Again	De novo	De-noh'voo
All	Todo	Toh'doo
Almost	Quase	Kwah'ze
Also	Tambem	Tan-ben
Although	Embora	En-bo'ra
Always	Sempre	Sen'pre
And	E	Ee
A, an	Um, uma	Oon, oona
Because	Porque	Poor'ke
Before	Antes	Antsh
Big	Grande	Grand
But	Mas	Mash
Can (I can)	Posso	Possoh
Come (I come)	Venho	Vain'yoh
Either/or	Um ou outro	Oon oh oh'troo
Find (I find)	Acho	Ash'oh
First	Primeiro	Pri-may'ee-roo
For	Para	Pa'ra
Friend		
From	De	Deh
Good	Bom	Bon
Goodbye	Adeus	A-day'oosh
Happy		
Have (I have)	Tenho	Tain'yoh
He	Ele	El'ay
Hello	Ola	O-lah

111

English	Portuguese	Portuguese Pronunciation
Here	Aqui	A-kee
I	Eu	Eh'oh
I am	Sou	Sue
If	Se	Seh
In	Em	En
Know (I know)	Conheco	Con'ye'soh
Last	Ultimo	Ool'tee-moo
Like (I like)	Gosto	Gos'toh
Little	Pequeno	Pe-kay'noo
Love (I love)		
Many	Muitos	Mween'toos
Me	Me	Meh
More	Mais	My'sh
Most	O mais	Ooh my'sh
Mr	Senhor	Se-nuohr
Much	Muito	Mween'too
My	Meu	May'oo
Never	Nunca	Noon'ka
New	Novo	Noh'voo
Next	Proximo	Pro'see-moo
No	Nao	Nown
Not	Nao	Nown
Now	Agora	A-go'ra
Of	De	Deh
Often	Muitas vezes	Mwee'tas vay'ze
Old	Velho	Ve'lyoo
On	Sobre	Soh'breh
One	Um, uma	Oon, oona
Only	Unico	Oo'nee-koo
Or	Ou	Oh
Other	Outro	Oh'troo
Our	Nosso	Nos'soh
Out	Fora	Fo'ra
Over	Sobre	Soh'breh
Part	Parte	Part
People	Gente	Zhent
Place	Lugar	Loo-gar
Please	Faca favor	Fassa fa-vohr
Same	Mesmo	Mayzh'moo
See (I see)	Vejo	Vay'yoh
She	Ela	Ella
So	Tao	Town
Some	Algum	Al-goon

112

English	Portuguese	Portuguese Pronunciation
Sometimes	Algumas vezes	Al'goo'mas vay'ze
Still	Mas	Mash
Such	Tal	Tal
Than	Que	Kay
Thank you	Obrigado	Oh-bree-gah'doo
That	Aquele	A'kay'le
The	O' a	Oh, ah
Their	Deles, delas, seu	Del'lays, del'lass, say'oo
Them	Os, as	Ohs, ass
Then	Depois	De-poh'eesh
There is, There are	Ha	Ha
They	Eles, elas	El'ays, el'ass
Thing	Coisa	Koh'ee-za
Think (I think)	Julgo	Yulgo
This	Este, esta	Aysht, esh'ta
Through	Por	Poor
Time	Tempo	Ten'poo
To	Para	Pa'ra
Under	Sob	Sohb
Up	Acima	A-see'ma
Us	Nos	Noh's
Use (I use)	Uso	Yoo'soh
Very	Muito	Mween'too
We	Nos	Noss
What	O que	Oh ke
When	Quando	Kwan'doo
Where	Onde	Ond
With	Com	Kon
Yes	Sim	Seen
You	Voce	Vo-say
Your	O seu	Oh say'oo

English	Spanish	Spanish Pronunciation
After	Despues	Days-pues
Again	De nuevo	Day nway'vo
All	Todo	To'do
Almost	Casi	Ka'see
Also	Tambien	Tam-byayn
Although	Aunque	Own'kay

113

English	Spanish	Spanish Pronunciation
Always	Siempre	Syem'pray
And	Y	Ee
A, an	Un, uno, una	Oon, oo'no, oo'na
Because	Porque	Por'kay
Before	Ante	An'tay
Big	Grande	Gran'day
But	Pero	Pay'ro
Can (I can)	Puedo	Pway'do
Come (I come)	Vengo	Ven'go
Either/or	O/o	Oh/oh
Find (I find)	Encuentro	En-kwen'tro
First	Primero	Pree-may'ro
For	Por	Por
Friend	Amigo	Ah'mee-goa
From	De	Day
Good	Bueno	Bway'no
Goodbye	Adios	Ah'dyos
Happy	Contento	Cont'ten'to
Have (I have)	Tengo	Tayn-go
He	El	Ell
Hello	Buenas dias	Bway'nas dee'as
Here	Aqui	Ah-kee
I	Yo	Yo
I am	Soy	Soy
If	Si	See
In	En	En
Know (I know)	Sabo	Sa-bo
Last	Ultimo	Ool'tee-mo
Like (I like)	Gusto	Goos-to
Little	Poco	Po'ko
Love (I love)	Amo	Ah'mo
Many	Muchos	Moo'chos
Me	Me	May
More	Mas	Mas
Most	Lo mas	Lo mas
Mr	Senor	Say-nyor
Much	Mucho	Moo'cho
My	Mi	Mee
Never	Nunca	Noon'ka
New	Nuevo	Nway'vo
Next	Proximo	Prok'see-mo
No	No	No
Not	No	No

English	Spanish	Spanish Pronunciation
Now	Ahora	Ah-o'ra
Of	De	Day
Often	Frecuentemente	Fray-kwen'tay' men'tay
Old	Viejo	Vy-ay'ho
On	Sobre	So'bray
One	Uno	Oo'no
Only	Solo	So'lo
Or	O	O
Other	Otro	O'tro
Our	Nuestro	Nway'stro
Out	Fuera	Fway'ra
Over	Sobre	So'bray
Part	Parte	Par'tay
People	Gente	Hen'tay
Place	Lugar	Loo-gar
Please	Por favor	Por fa'vor
Same	Mismo	Mees'mo
See (I see)	Veo	Vay'o
She	Ella	El'lya
So	Asi	Ah-see
Some	Algun	Al-goon
Sometimes	Alguna vez	Al-goo'na vayth
Still	Siempre	Syem'pray
Such	Tal	Tal
Than	Que	Kay
Thank you	Gracias	Gra'thyas
That	Ese	Ay'say
The	El, la, lo	Ayl, lah, loh
Their	Su, sus	Soo, soos
Them	Los, las, les	Loss, lahss, lays
Then	Luego	Lway'go
There is, There are	Hay	Ahy
They	Ellos, ellas	Ay'lyos, Ay,lyahss
Thing	Cosa	Ko'sa
Think (I think)	Pienso	Pyayn-so
This	Este, esta	Ays'tay, ays'tah
Through	Por	Por
Time	Tiempo	Tyem'po
To	A	Ah
Under	Debajo	Day-ba'ho
Up	Arriba	Ah-ree'ba
Us	Nos	Nohs

English	Spanish	Spanish Pronunciation
Use (I use)	Uso	Oo'so
Very	Mismo	Mees'mo
We	Nosotros	Nohs'ot'rohs
What	Lo que	Lo kay
When	Cuando	kwan'do
Where	Donde	Don'day
With	Con	Kon
Yes	Si	See
You	Tu	Too
Your	Suyo	Soo'yo

English	Russian	Russian Pronunciation
After	Posle	Poh'slyeh
Again	Yeshcho	Yesh-choh
All	Vsye	Fsyeh
Almost	Pochti	Puhch-tee
Also	Tozhe	Toh'zheh
Although	Khotya	Khot-yah
Always	Vsyegda	Fsyeg-dah
And	I	Ee
A, an	–	–
Because	Potomu chto	Puh-tom-oo shtoh
Before	Do	Doh
Big	Bolshoi	Bul-shoy
But	No	No
Can (I can)	Ya mogu	Yah mug-oo
Come (I come)	Ya pridu	Yah pree-doo
Either/or	Ili/ili	Ee'li/ee'li
Find (I find)	Ya naidu	Yah nah-ee-doo
First	Pervyi	Pyehr Vooee
For	Dlya	Dlyah
Friend	Dryg	Droog
From	Ot	Ot
Good	Khorosho	Khuh-rah-shoh
Goodbye	Do svidanya	Duh-svid-ahn'yah
Happy	Shastlivi	Shast'lee-vee
Have (I have)	Ya imyeyu	Yah eem-yay'yoo
He	On	Ohn
Hello	Sdravstvuitye	Zdrahfst'voo-it-yeh
Here	Zdyes	Zdyehs

116

English	Russian	Russian Pronunciation
I	Ya	Yah
I am	Ya	Yah
If	Yesli	Yes'lee
In	V	V
Know (I know)	Ya znayu	Yah Znaee'yoo
Last	Poslyedni	Puh'slyay'dnee
Like (I like)	Mnye nravitsya	Mnyeh'nrah'vits-yah
Little	Malyenki	Mahl'yenkee
Love (I love)	Ya lyooblyoo	Yah lyoo'blyoo
Many	Mhogo	Mnoh'goh
Me	Menya	Men-yah
More	Bolshe	Bohl'shyeh
Most	Nai-bolshi	Nahee-bohl'shee
Mr	Gospodin	Guhs-pah-deen
Much	Mnogo	Mnoh'goh
My	Moi	Mo'ee
Never	Nikogda	Nee-kuhg-dah
New	Novyi	Noh'vooee
Next	Slyeduyushchi	Slyed'ooyoo-shchee
No	Nyet	Nyet
Not	Nye	Nyeh
Now	Tepyer	Tip-yehr
Of	Iz	Is
Often	Chasto	Chuh'stoh
Old	Staryi	Stah'rooee
On	Na	Nah
One	Odin	Uh-deen
Only	Tolko	Tohl'koh
Or	Ili	Ee'li
Other	Drugoi	Droo-goy
Our	Nash	Nahsh
Out	Iz	Is
Over	Nad	Nahd
Part	Chast	Chahst
People	Lyudi	Lyoo'dee
Place	Myesto	Myes'toh
Please	Pozhaluista	Puh-zhahl'stah
Same	Samyi	Sahm'ooee
See (I see)	Ya Vizhu	Yah vee'zhoo
She	Ona	Uh-nah
So	Tak	Tunk
Some	Nyekotoryi	Nyeh'kuh-toh-rooee
Sometimes	Inogda	Ee-nuhg-dah

English	Russian	Russian Pronunciation
Still	Yeshcho	Yesh-choh
Such	Takoi	Tuh-koy
Than	Chem	Chem
Thank you	Spasibo	Spuh-see'buh
That	Etot	Eh'tuht
The	–	–
Their	Ikh	Eekh
Them	Ikh	Eekh
Then	Togda	Tuhg-dah
There is, There are	Yest	Yehst
They	Oni	Uh-nee
Thing	Predmyet	Pred-myet
Think (I think)	Ya dumayu	Yah doo'mah-yoo
This	Etot	Eh'tuht
Through	Cherez	Cheh'rez
Time	Vremya	Vrhh'myah
To	Na	Nah
Under	Pod	Pod
Up	Naverkh	Nah-vehrkh
Us	Nas	Nahs
Use (I use)	Ya ispolsuyu	Yah is-pol'zoo-yoo
Very	Ochen	Oh'chen
We	Myi	Mooee
What	Chto	Shtoh
When	Kogda	Kuhg-dah
Where	Gdye	Gdyeh
With	S	S
Yes	Da	Dah
You	Vyi	Vooee
Your	Vash	Vahsh

English	Swedish	Swedish Pronunciation
After	Efter	Ef'ter
Again	Igen	Ee-yan
All	All	Al
Almost	Naestan	Nast-an
Also	Ocksaa	Oxo
Although	Aeven om	Air-ven om
Always	Alltid	Ull-tid
And	Och	Ok

English	Swedish	Swedish Pronunciation
A, an	En, ett	En, et
Because	Daerfoer att	Dair-fuhr art
Before	Innan	In-nan
Big	Stor	Storr
But	Men	Men
Can (I can)	Jag kan	Jarg kan
Come (I come)	Jag kommer	Jarg kom-merr
Either/or	Antingen/eller	An-ting-en/ell-err
Find (I find)	Jag finner	Jarg fin-nerr
First	Foerst	Firsht
For	Foer	Furr
Friend	Vaen	Ven
From	Fraan	Frorn
Good	Bra	Bra
Goodbye	Adjoe	Ad-jo
Happy	Glad	Glard
Have (I have)	Jag har	Jarg harr
He	Han	Hun
Hello	Goddag	Go-darg
Here	Haer	Harr
I	Jag	Jarg
I am	Jag aer	Jarg arr
If	Om	Om
In	I	Ee
Know (I know)	Jag kan	Jarg kan
Last	Foerra	For-rah
Like (I like)	Jag tycker om	Jarg tickerr om
Little	Liten, Litet	Litten, littett
Love (I love)	Jag Aelskar	Jarg elskarr
Many	Manga	Mong'a
Me	Mig	May
More	Mera	Meer-ra
Most	Mest	Mest
Mr	Herr	Herr
Much	Mycket	Micket
My	Min, Mitt	Min, mitt
Never	Aldrig	All-drig
New	Ny	Nu
Next	Naesta	Nest
No	Nej	Nay
Not	Inte	Inter
Now	Nu	Nu
Of	Av	Arv

English	Swedish	Swedish Pronunciation
Often	Ofta	Ofta
Old	Gammal	Gam'marl
On	Paa	Por
One	En, ett, man	En, ett, man
Only	Bara	Bar'ra
Or	Eller	Ellerr
Other	Annan, Annat	Annan, annat
Our	Vaar, Vaart, Vaara	Vorr, vorrt, vorr'ah
Out	Ut	Uut
Over	Over	Er-ver
Part	Del	Dail
People	Folk	Folk
Place	Plats	Plats
Please	Varsaagod	Vor-so-good
Same	Samma	Sam'ma
See (I see)	Jag ser	Jarg seer
She	Hon	Hon
So	Saa	Sor
Some	Naagon, Naagot, Naagra	No'gon, No'got, No'grra
Sometimes	Ibland	Ee'bland
Still	Aendaa	An'dor
Such	Saadan	Sor'dan
Than	Aen	An
Thank you	Tack	Tack
That	Att	At
The	–	–
Their	Deras	Dair'as
Them	Dem	Dem
Then	Daa	Dor
There is, There are	Det finns, det ar	Det fins, det air
They	De	Dear
Thing	Sak	Sark
Think (I think)	Jag tror	Jarg trorr
This	Denna, detta	Denna, detta
Through	Genom	Je'nom
Time	Tid	Teed
To	Till	Till
Under	Under	Onderr
Up	Upp	Opp
Us	Oss	Oss
Use (I use)	Jag anvaender	Jarg an'van-derr
Very	Mycket	Micket

English	Swedish	Swedish Pronunciation
We	Vi	Vee
What	Vad	Vard
When	Naer	Nair
Where	Var	Varr
With	Med	Maird
Yes	Ja	Ja
You	Du, ni	Duu, nee
Your	Din, ditt	Din, ditt

NOTES ON SWEDISH TRANSLATION
AA=Å
AE=Ä
OE=Ö

English	Chinese (Ping Yin)	Chinese (Ping Yin) Pronunciation
After	Guo le	Gwo le
Again	You	Yoh
All	Dou	Doh
Almost	Cha bu duo	Chah boo dwoh
Also	Hai	Hih
Although	Sui ran	Sway rran
Always	Yong yuan	Yung yooen
And	He	He
A, an	Yi ge	Ee ge
Because	Yin wei	Yin way
Before	Yi oian	Ee chen
Big	Da	Dah
But	Ke shi	Ke she
Can (I can)	Ke yi	Ke ee
Come (I come)	Lai	Lih
Either/or	Huo zhe	Hwoh je
Find (I find)	Zhou dao	Joh dow
First	De yi	De ee
For	Wei	Way
Friend	Paang-yau	Peng ee-oo
From	Cong	Tsong
Good	Hao	How
Goodbye	Cai jain	Tsih jen
Happy	Xin-fu	Shing-fu

121

English	Chinese (Ping Yin)	Chinese (Ping Yin) Pronunciation
Have (I have)	You	Yoh
He	Ta	Tah
Hello	Ni hao	Nee how
Here	Zher	Jer
I	Wo	Woh
I am	Wo shi	Woh she
If	Ru guo	Rroo gwoh
In	Li	Lee
Know (I know)	Zhe dao	Je dow
Last	Zui hou	Dzway hoh
Like (I like)	Ai	Ih
Little	Xiao	Seeow
Love (I love)	Wo ai	War ah
Many	Duo	Dwoh
Me	Wo	Woh
More	Duo	Dwoh
Most	Zui duo	Dzway dwoh
Mr	Xienxing	See-en sing
Much	Duo	Dwoh
My	Wo de	Woh de
Never	Zong bu	Dzong boo
New	Xin	Sin
Next	Pang bian	Pung bee-en
No	Bu shi	Boo she
Not	Bu	Boo
Now	Xian zai	See'en tsih
Of	De	De
Often	Chang chang	Chang chang
Old	Lao	Low
On	Zai	Tsih
One	Yi	Ee
Only	Zhi	Je
Or	Hai shi	Hih she
Other	Bie de	Beeye de
Our	Wo men de	Woh men de
Out	Wai	Wih
Over	Shiang	Seeyang
Part	Bu fen	Boo fen
People	Ren	Rren
Place	Di fang	Dee fang
Please	Qing	Ching
Same	Tong	Tung
See (I see)	Kan jian	Kan jen

English	Chinese (Ping Yin)	Chinese (Ping Yin) Pronunciation
She	Ta	Tah
So	Suo yi	Soowoh ee
Some	Yi xie	Ee sye
Sometimes	You shi huo	Yoh she hwoh
Still	Hai	Hih
Such	Na me	Nah me
Than	Bi	Bee
Thank you	Xie xie	Sye sye
That	Na ge	Nah ge
The	–	–
Their	Ta men de	Tah men de
Them	Ta men	Tah men
Then	Ran hou	Rran hoh
There is, There are	You	Yoh
They	Ta men	Tah men
Thing	Dong xi	Dung see
Think (I think)	Xiang	Seeyang
This	Zhei ge	Jay ge
Through	Tong guo	Tung gwoh
Time	Shi jian	She jen
To	Dao	Dow
Under	Xia	Seeah
Up	Shiang	Sheeang
Us	Wo men	Woh men
Use (I use)	Yong	Yung
Very	Hen	Hen
We	Wo men	Woh men
What	Shen me	She me
When	Shen me shi hou	She me she hoh
Where	Zai nar	Tsih nar
With	Tong	Tung
Yes	Shi	She
You	Ni	Nee
Your	Ni de	Nee de

English	Japanese	Japanese Pronunciation
After	Atode	Ah-toh-deh
Again	Mata	Mah-tah
All	Minna	Meen-nah
Almost	Hotondo	Hoh-tohn-doh

English	Japanese	Japanese Pronunciation
Also	Mata	Mah-tah
Although	Keredomo	Keh-reh-doh-moh
Always	Itsumo	Ee-tsoo-moh
And	Soshite	Soh-shee-teh
A, an	Hitotsu no	Hee-toh-tsoo noh
Because	Node	Noh-deh
Before	Mae ni	Mah-eh nee
Big	Okii	Oh-kee
But	Keredomo	Keh-reh-doh-moh
Can (I can)	Dekiru	Deh-kee-doo
Come (I come)	Kuru	Koo-doo
Either/or	Ka	Kah
Find (I find)	Mitsukeru	Mee-tsoo-keh-doo
First	Hajime	Hah-jee-meh
For	Tamini	Tah-mee-nee
Friend	Tomodachi	Tomo-dar'chee
From	Kara	Kah-dah
Good	Ii	Ee
Goodbye	Sayonara	Sah-yoh-nah-dah
Happy	Shiawase	Shee'a-wah'say
Have (I have)	Motte imasu	Moht-teh ee-mahss
He	Kare	Kah-deh
Hello	Konnichi wa	Kohn-nee-chee wah
Here	Koko	Koh-koh
I	Watashi	Wah-tah-shee
I am	Watashi wa	Wah-tah-shee wah
If	Moshi	Moh-shee
In	Ni	Nee
Know (I know)	Shitte imasu	Sheet-teh ee-mahss
Last	Owari	Oh-wah-dee
Like (I like)	Suki	Soo-kee
Little	Chiisai	Chee-sah-ee
Love (I love)	Sukidesu	Soo'kee-dess'oo
Many	Takusan	Tah-koo-sahn
Me	Watashi ni	Wah-tah-shee nee
More	Motto	Moht-toh
Most	Ichidan	Ee-chee-bahn
Mr	San	Sahn
Much	Takusan	Tah-koo-sahn
My	Watashi no	Wah-tah-shee noh
Never	Dekinai	Deh-kee-nah-ee
New	Atarashii	Ah-tah-dah-shee
Next	Tonari	Toh-nah-dee

124

English	Japanese	Japanese Pronunciation
No	Iie	Ee-eh
Not	Shinai	Shee-nah-ee
Now	Ima	Ee-mah
Of	No	Noh
Often	Tabitabi	Tah-bee-tah-bee
Old	Toshiyori	Toh-shee-yoh-dee
On	Ue	Oo-eh
One	Ichi	Ee-chee
Only	Tatta	Taht-tah
Or	Ka	Kah
Other	Hoka	Hoh-kah
Our	Watatshitachi no	Wah-tah-shee-tah-chee noh
Out	Soto	Soh-toh
Over	Ue	Oo-eh
Part	Ichibu	Ee-chee-boo
People	Hitobito	Hee-toh-bee-toh
Place	Tokoro	Toh-koh-doh
Please	Kudasai	Koo-dah-sich
Same	Onaji	Oh-noh-jee
See (I see)	Mimasu	Mee-mahss
She	Kanojo	Kah-noh-joh
So	So	Soh
Some	Ikuraka	Ee-koo-dah-kah
Sometimes	Tokidoki	Toh-kee-doh-kee
Still	Mada	Mah-dah
Such	Sonna	Sohn-nah
Than	Yori	Yoh-dee
Thank you	Arigato	Ah-dee-gah-toh
That	Sono	Soh-noh
The	Sono	Soh-noh
Their	Karera no	Kah-deh-dah noh
Them	Karera no	Kah-deh-dah noh
Then	Dewa	Deh-wah
There is, There are	Soko desu	Soh-koh dess
They	Karera	Kah-deh-dah
Thing	Mono	Moh-noh
Think (I think)	Omou	Oh-moh-oo
This	Kono	Koh-noh
Through	Toru	Toh-doo
Time	Jikan	Jee-kahn
To	Ni	Nee
Under	Shita	Shee-tah

125

English	Japanese	Japanese Pronunciation
Up	Ue	Oo-eh
Us	Wareware ni	Wah-deh-wah-deh nee
Use (I use)	Tsukau	Tsoo-kah-oo
Very	Taihen	Tie-hehn
We	Watashitachi	Wah-tah-shee-tah-chee
What	Nani	Nah-nee
When	Itsu	Ee-tsoo
Where	Doko	Doh-koh
With	De	Deh
Yes	Hai	Hie
You	Anata	Ah-nah-tah
Your	Anata no	Ah-nah-tah noh

English	Esperanto	Esperanto Pronunciation
After	Post	Post
Again	Denove	De-nor've
All	Tuto	Too'tor
Almost	Preskau	Pres'kow
Also	Ankau	Ahn'kow
Although	Kvankam	Kvun'kum
Always	Ciam	Chee'um
And	Kaj	K'eye
A, an	–	–
Because	Car	Churr
Before	Antau	Anh'tow
Big	Granda	Grun'dah
But	Sed	Sed
Can (I can)	Mi povas	Mee por'vus
Come (I come)	Mi venas	Mee ven'us
Either/or	Au/au	Ow ow
Find (I find)	Mi trovas	Mee tror'vus
First	Unua	Oo-noo'ah
For	Por	Porr
Friend	Amiko	Ah-mee'kor
From	De	Deh
Good	Bona	Bor'nah
Goodbye	Gis la revido	Jeess lah re-vee'dor
Happy	Felica	Fell-eetch'ah
Have (I have)	Mi havas	Mee hah'vus

126

English	Esperanto	Esperanto Pronunciation
He	Li	Lee
Hello	Saluton	Sul-oo'ton
Here	Tie ci	Tee'eh chee
I	Me	Mee
I am	Mi estas	Mee ess'tus
If	Se	Seh
In	En	Enn
Know (I know)	Mi scias	Mee stsee'us
Last	Lasta	Luss'tah
Like (I like)	Mi satas	Mee shah'tus
Little	Malgranda	Mul-grun'dah
Love (I love)	Mi amas	Mee ahm'us
Many	Multaj	Mool-t'eye
Me	Min	Meen
More	Pli	Plee
Most	Plej	Play
Mr	Sinjoro	Shen-yor'or
Much	Multo	Mool'tor
My	Mia	Mee'ah
Never	Neniam	Nen-ee'um
New	Nova	Nor'vah
Next	Venonta	Ven-on'tah
No	Ne	Neh
Not	Ne	Neh
Now	Nun	Noon
Of	De	Deh
Often	Ofte	Offt'ay
Old	Maljuna	Mull-yoo'nah
On	Sur	Soor
One	Unu	Oo'noo
Only	Nur	Noor
Or	Au	Ow
Other	Alia	Ul-ee'ah
Our	Nia	Nee'ah
Out	El	El
Over	Super	Soo'payr
Part	Parto	Purr'toh
People	Homoj	Hor'moy
Place	Loko	Lor'kor
Please	Bonvolu	Bon-vor'loo
Same	Sama	Sah'mah
See (I see)	Mi vidas	Mee vee'dus
She	Si	She

English	Esperanto	Esperanto Pronunciation
So	Tiel	Tee'el
Some	Kelkaj	Kel'kay
Sometimes	Kelkfoje	Kelk-foy'ay
Still	Ankorau	Unk-or-ow
Such	Tiel	Tee'el
Than	Ol	Ol
Thank you	Dankon	Dun'kon
That	Ke	Kay
The	La	Lah
Their	Ilia	Ill-ee'ah
Them	Ilin	Ill'een
Then	Tiam	Tee'um
There is, There are	Jen	Yen
They	Ili	Ee'lee
Thing	Ajo	Ah'zho
Think (I think)	Mi pensas	Mee pen'sus
This	Tiu ci	Tee'oo chee
Through	Tra	Trah
Time	Tempo	Tem'por
To	Al	Ull
Under	Sub	Soob
Up	Supren	Soop'ren
Us	Nin	Neen
Use (I use)	Mi uzas	Mee ooz'us
Very	Tre	Tray
We	Ni	Nee
What	Kio	Kee'or
When	Kiam	Kee'm
Where	Kie	Kee'ay
With	Kun	Koon
Yes	Jes	Yes
You	Vi	Vee
Your	Via	Vee'ah

CHAPTER TEN

COUNTRIES/CAPITALS

Country	*Capital*
Afghanistan	Kabul
Albania	Tirane
Algeria	Algiers
Andorra	Andorra
Angola	Luanda
Argentina	Buenos Aires
Australia	Canberra
Austria	Vienna
Bahamas	Nassau
Bahrain	Manama
Bangladesh	Dhaka
Belgium	Brussels
Belize	Belmopan
Benin	Porto Novo
Bolivia	La Paz
Botswana	Gaborone
Brazil	Brasilia
Brunei	Bandar Seri Begawan
Bulgaria	Sofia
Burkina	Quagadougou
Burma	Rangoon
Burundi	Bujumbura
Cambodia	Phnom Penh
Cameroon	Yaounde
Canada	Ottawa
Central African Republic	Bangui
Chad	N'djamena
Chile	Santiago
China	Beijing
Colombia	Bogota
Comoros	Moroni
Congo	Brazzaville
Costa Rica	San Jose
Cuba	Havana
Cyprus	Nicosia

Country	Capital
Czechoslovakia	Prague
Denmark	Copenhagen
Djibouti	Djibouti
Dominican Republic	Santo Domingo
East Germany	Berlin
Ecuador	Quito
Egypt	Cairo
El Salvador	San Salvador
Equatorial Guinea	Malabo
Ethiopia	Addis Ababa
Falkland Islands	Stanley
Finland	Helsinki
France	Paris
French Guiana	Cayenne
Gabon	Libreville
Gambia	Banjul
Ghana	Accra
Greece	Athens
Guatemala	Guatemala
Guinea	Conakry
Guinea-Bissau	Bissau
Guyana	Georgetown
Haiti	Port au Prince
Honduras	Tegucigalpa
Hungary	Budapest
Iceland	Reykjavik
India	New Delhi
Indonesia	Java
Iran	Tehran
Iraq	Baghdad
Ireland	Dublin
Israel	Jerusalem
Italy	Rome
Ivory Coast	Abidjan
Jamaica	Kingston
Japan	Tokyo
Jordan	Amman
Kenya	Nairobi
Kuwait	Kuwait
Laos	Vientiane
Lebanon	Beirut
Lesotho	Maseru
Liberia	Monrovia
Libya	Tripoli

Country	Capital
Liechtenstein	Vaduz
Luxembourg	Luxembourg
Madagascar	Antananarivo
Malawi	Lilongwe
Malaysia	Kuala Lumpur
Maldives	Male
Mali	Bamako
Malta	Valleta
Mauritania	Nouakchott
Mexico	Mexico City
Monaco	Monaco
Mongolia	Ulaanbaatar
Morocco	Rabat
Mozambique	Maputo
Namibia	Windhoek
Nepal	Katmandu
Netherlands	Amsterdam
New Zealand	Wellington
Nicaragua	Managua
Niger	Niamey
Nigeria	Lagos
North Korea	Pyongyang
Norway	Oslo
Oman	Muscat
Pakistan	Islamabad
Panama	Panama
Papua New Guinea	Port Moresby
Paraguay	Asuncion
Peru	Lima
Philippines	Manila
Poland	Warsaw
Portugal	Lisbon
Puerto Rico	San Juan
Qatar	Doha
Romania	Bucharest
Rwanda	Kigali
Sao Tome & Principe	Sao Tome
Saudi Arabia	Riyadh
Senegal	Dakar
Sierra Leone	Freetown
Singapore	Singapore
Somalia	Mogadishu
South Africa	Pretoria
South Korea	Seoul

Country	Capital
Soviet Union	Moscow
Spain	Madrid
Sri Lanka	Colombo
Sudan	Khartoum
Suriname	Paramaribo
Swaziland	Mbabane
Sweden	Stockholm
Switzerland	Bern
Syria	Damascus
Taiwan	Taipei
Tanzania	Dar es Salaam
Thailand	Bangkok
Togo	Lome
Trinidad & Tobago	Port of Spain
Tunisia	Tunis
Turkey	Ankara
Uganda	Kampala
United Arab Emirates	Abu Dhabi
United Kingdom	London
United States	Washington
Uruguay	Montevideo
Venezuela	Caracas
Vietnam	Hanoi
West Germany	Bonn
Yemen	San'a
Yemen (P.D.R. of)	Aden
Yugoslavia	Belgrade
Zaire	Kinshasa
Zambia	Lusaka
Zimbabwe	Harare

CHAPTER ELEVEN

KINGS AND QUEENS OF ENGLAND

	from	*to*		*from*	*to*
William I	1066	1087	Jane	1553	
William II	1087	1100	Mary I	1553	1558
Henry I	1100	1135	Elizabeth I	1558	1603
Stephen	1135	1154	James I	1603	1625
Henry II	1154	1189	Charles I	1625	1649
Richard I	1189	1199	Charles II	1660	1685
John	1199	1216	James II	1685	1688
Henry III	1216	1272	William III and	1688	1702
Edward I	1272	1307	Mary II	1688	1694
Edward II	1307	1327	Anne	1702	1714
Edward III	1327	1377	George I	1714	1727
Richard II	1377	1399	George II	1727	1760
Henry IV	1399	1413	George III	1760	1820
Henry V	1413	1422	George IV	1820	1830
Henry VI	1422	1461	William IV	1830	1837
Edward IV	1461	1483	Victoria	1837	1901
Edward V	1483		Edward VII	1901	1910
Richard III	1483	1485	George V	1910	1936
Henry VII	1485	1509	Edward VIII	1936	
Henry VIII	1509	1547	George VI	1936	1952
Edward VI	1547	1553	Elizabeth II	1952	

CHAPTER TWELVE

ELEMENTS

The names of the various families or groupings of the elements are abbreviations of the following:

Hydrogen	Hydrogen
Noble Gases	Noble Gases
Alkaline	Alkali and Alkaline Earth Metals
Boron/Carbon	Boron and Carbon Families
Nitrogen/Oxygen	Nitrogen and Oxygen Families
The Halogens	The Halogens
Early Trans Metals	Early Transition Metals
Late Trans Metals	Late Transition Metals
The Triads	The Triads
Rare Earth Metals	Rare Earth Metals
Actinide	Actinide Metals

Atomic Number	*Element*	*Symbol*	*Atomic Weight*	*Family*
1	HYDROGEN	H	1.008	HYDROGEN

From hydor and gen, or water-forming; discovered in 1766; third most abundant and lightest element. Hydrogen is almost never found free on earth, but the sun and other stars are almost pure hydrogen. The thermonuclear fusion of hydrogen nuclei lights and heats the universe.

2	HELIUM	He	4.0026	NOBLE GASES

From helios, or sun; discovered in 1868; almost all the helium in the world comes from natural gas wells in the United States. One well in Arizona produces a gas that is 8% helium. Lighter than air, it is widely used in balloons in place of highly inflammable hydrogen.

3	LITHIUM	Li	6.941	ALKALINE

From lithos, discovered in 1817; the lightest of the solid elements. Lithium forms a black oxide when exposed to air. It is used in ceramics, alloys, in the H-bomb – and in treating both gout victims and manic-depressives.

Atomic Number	Element	Symbol	Atomic Weight	Family
4	BERYLLIUM	Be	9.012	ALKALINE

From the mineral beryl, in which it was found in 1798. This element produces alloys that are extremely elastic, hence its role in making gears, springs and other machine parts. Because of its high melting point – 1,285°C – beryllium goes into making rocket nose cones.

5	BORON	B	10.811	BORON/CARBON

From borax and carbon; discovered 1808. A non-metal, boron is best known in borax (sodium borate) and in boric-acid – the one acid that is good for the eyes. About a million tons of boron are used in industry each year. In agriculture it serves as both a plant food and a weed killer.

6	CARBON	C	12.011	BORON/CARBON

From carbo, or charcoal; prehistoric. Carbon, in its endless variety of compounds, is an indispensable source of everyday products, such as nylon and petrol, perfume and plastics, shoe polish, DDT and TNT.

7	NITROGEN	N	14.007	NITROGEN/OXYGEN

From nitron and gen, or nitre-forming; discovered in 1772; a gas making up 78% of the air. Nitrogen can be 'fixed' from the air – compounds include the anaesthetic 'laughing gas', explosives such as TNT, fertilisers, and amino-acids – the building blocks of protein.

8	OXYGEN	O	15.999	NITROGEN/OXYGEN

From oxys and gen, or acid-forming; discovered in 1774; the most abundant element, making up about half of everything on earth, 21% of the atmosphere by volume and two-thirds of the human body. Breathed in by animals, oxygen is restored to the air by plants.

9	FLUORINE	F	18.998	HALOGENS

From fluo, or flow; discovered 1771. Fluorine is the most reactive of the non-metals; only a few of the inert gases resist it. It corrodes platinum, a material that withstands most other chemicals. In a stream of fluorine gas, wood and rubber burst into flame – and even asbestos glows.

10	NEON	Ne	20.183	NOBLE GASES

From neos, or new; discovered 1898. The best known of the inert gases, it is chiefly used in advertising. The ubiquitous 'neon sign' is a glass vacuum tube containing a minute amount of neon gas; when an electric current is passed through, the tube gives off a bright orange-red light.

Atomic Number	Element	Symbol	Atomic Weight	Family
11	SODIUM	Na	22.990	ALKALINE

From soda; symbol from its Latin name Natrium; discovered 1807; sixth most abundant element. Metallic sodium is too violent for most everyday uses and is generally stored in paraffin. But its useful compounds include table salt, baking soda, borax and lye.

12	MAGNESIUM	Mg	24.3	ALKALINE

From Magnesia, an ancient city in Asia Minor; discovered 1775; eighth most abundant element; burns as a powder or foil in fire-crackers, bombs, and flash bulbs. It has one odd biological effect: a deficiency in man can have the same effect as alcoholism, delirium tremens.

13	ALUMINIUM	Al	26.982	BORON/CARBON

From alumen, or alum; discovered 1827; the most abundant metal and third most abundant element, its uses range from toothpaste tubes to aeroplane wings. Early samples cost £230 per pound; now over a million tons are produced yearly in the U.S. for as low as £0.30 per pound.

14	SILICON	Si	28.086	BORON/CARBON

From silex, or flint; discovered 1823; the second most abundant element – making up one-quarter of the earth's crust. Sand, largely silicon dioxide, goes into making glass and cement. Pure silicon is used in micro-electronic devices such as solar batteries to power satellite instruments.

15	PHOSPHORUS	P	30.974	NITROGEN/OXYGEN

From phosphoros, or light bearer; discovered 1669; occurs in three major forms – white, red and rarely black. The white so unstable that it yellows then reddens in light, glows in the dark – hence 'phosphorescence'. Phosphates are ingredients of detergents.

16	SULPHUR	S	32.064	NITROGEN/OXYGEN

From sulphur, or brimstone its biblical name; recognised since ancient times. Used in all branches of modern industry, it turns up among other places in matches, insecticides and rubber tyres. Nearly 200 pounds of sulphuric acid per capita are produced in the U.S. each year.

17	CHLORINE	Cl	35.453	HALOGENS

From chloros, or greenish-yellow; discovered 1774. Combining with almost as many elements as fluorine, chlorine is less corrosive but strong enough to be used as a bleach, a disinfectant and a poison gas. Pure chlorine is commonly prepared from ordinary salt.

Atomic Number	Element	Symbol	Atomic Weight	Family

18   ARGON   Ar   39.948   NOBLE GASES
From argon, or inactive; discovered 1894. The most abundant of noble gases, argon makes up 0.934% of the air. Its industrial forte is in welding; it provides an inert atmosphere in which welded metals will not burn. It is also the gas that fills ordinary incandescent light bulbs.

19   POTASSIUM   K   39.1   ALKALINE
From potash, an impure form of potassium carbonate known to the ancients; symbol K from its Latin name kalium; discovered 1807. Seventh most abundant element in the earth's crust. Its radioactivity, though mild, may be one natural cause of genetic mutation in man.

20   CALCIUM   Ca   40.08   ALKALINE
From calx, or lime – an oxide of calcium; discovered 1808; fifth most abundant in the earth's crust. Its presence in our bodies is essential. Normal quota in an adult is about 2 pounds, mostly in the teeth and bones. Calcium also plays a role in regulating the heartbeat.

21   SCANDIUM   Sc   44.956   EARLY TRANS METALS
From Scandinavia; discovered 1879. Although no practical uses have yet been found for this metal, its potential is great because it is almost as light as aluminium and has a much higher melting point. A pound of scandium produced in 1960 was the first such quantity made.

22   TITANIUM   Ti   47.9   EARLY TRANS METALS
From Titans, the supermen of Greek myth; discovered in 1791. Although it is the ninth most abundant element, titanium has only begun to serve man. Its white dioxide goes into bright paints. The metal itself is used in constructing supersonic aircraft such as Concorde.

23   VANADIUM   V   50.942   EARLY TRANS METALS
From Vanadis, a Scandinavian goddess; discovered 1830. Added to steel, vanadium produces one of the toughest alloys for armour plate, axles, piston rods and crankshafts. Less than 1% of vanadium and a little chromium makes steel shock and vibration resistant.

24   CHROMIUM   Cr   51.996   EARLY TRANS METALS
From chroma, or colour; discovered 1797. A very bright silvery metal, it forms compounds valued as pigments for their vivid green, yellow, red and orange colours. The ruby takes its colour from chromium. Besides lustrous chrome plate, its alloys include a number of special hard steels.

Atomic Number	Element	Symbol	Atomic Weight	Family

25   MANGANESE   Mn   54.938   EARLY TRANS METALS
From magnes, or magnet – its ore was first confused with magnetic iron ore; discovered 1774. Manganese which gives steel a hard yet pliant quality, seems to play a similar role in animal bone: without it, bones grow spongier and break more easily. It activates many enzymes.

26   IRON   Fe   55.847   TRIADS
From iren, its old English name; symbol Fe from its latin name, ferrum; first utilised by prehistoric man. The fourth most abundant element and the cheapest metal, iron is the basic ingredient of all steel. Making up part of the compound haemoglobin, it carries oxygen in the blood stream.

27   COBALT   Co   58.933   TRIADS
From kobold, or evil spirit (its poisonous ores were once treacherous to mine); discovered 1735. For centuries cobalt's blue salts have given colour to porcelains, tiles and enamels. Its alloys go into making jet propulsion engines, and its radioactive isotope is used to treat cancer.

28   NICKEL   Ni   58.7   TRIADS
From the German Kupfernickel, or false copper, a reddish ore contain nickel but no copper; discovered 1751. Its hard durable qualities have long made nickel popular for coins – the U.S. 5 cent piece is 25% nickel, the rest copper. Nickel plate protects softer metals.

29   COPPER   Cu   63.5   LATE TRANS METALS
From cuprum, derived from the ancient name for Cyprus, famed for its copper mines; known by early man. It and gold are the only two coloured metals. Alloyed in most gold jewellery and silverware, copper is mixed with zinc in brass, with tin in bronze. A "copper" penny is bronze.

30   ZINC   Zn   65.38   LATE TRANS METALS
Probably from zin, German for tin; discovered by the alchemist Paracelsus in 16th century, though the zinc-copper alloy brass was known to the ancients. While not technically a coloured metal, zinc has a bluish cast. An excellent coating metal, it is used to line flashlight batteries.

31   GALLIUM   Ga   69.72   BORON/CARBON
From Gallia, the old name for France; discovered 1875. A metal that melts in the hand, it is one of the few that expands as it freezes, as do non-metals and most gases. Its high boiling point – 1,983°C – makes

Atomic			*Atomic*	
Number	*Element*	*Symbol*	*Weight*	*Family*

it ideal for recording temperatures that would vaporise a thermometer.

32	GERMANIUM	Ge	72.59	BORON/CARBON

From Germany; discovered 1886. The first metal in the carbon family, germanium resembles the non-metal silicon. The first element used for transistors, it has brought about the replacement of large vacuum tubes with devices 1/400″ across.

33	ARSENIC	As	74.933	NITROGEN/OXYGEN

From arsenikos, or male (the Greeks believed metals differed in sex); discovered about 1250. Best classed as a non-metal with a few metallic traits, arsenic is famed as a poison but some of its compounds are medicines. When heated it "sublimes" – i.e. the solid evaporises directly.

34	SELENIUM	Se	78.96	NITROGEN/OXYGEN

From selene, or moon; discovered 1817; exists both as metal and non-metal. Unlike most electrical conductors, selenium varies in conductivity with variations in light. This "photo-electric" trait suits it for service in electric eyes, solar cells, television cameras and light meters.

35	BROMINE	Br	79.9	HALOGENS

From bromos, or stench; discovered 1826; a red, caustic, fuming liquid, with a foul smell. Bromine is an effective disinfectant. Among its compounds are the bromides, used in nerve sedatives, and in petrol anti-knock compounds that make car engines run smoothly.

36	KRYPTON	Kr	83.8	NOBLE GASES

From kryptos, or hidden; discovered in 1898. Radioactive krypton is used to keep tabs on Soviet nuclear production. Because this gas is a by-product of all nuclear reactors, the Russian share is found by subtracting the amount that comes from Western reactors from the total in the air.

37	RUBIDIUM	Rb	85.47	ALKALINE

From rubidus, or red (the colour its salts impart to flames); discovered 1861. Used in electric eye-cells, also a potential space fuel. Like potassium, it is slightly radioactive, and has been used to locate brain tumours, as it collects in tumours but not in normal tissue.

38	STRONTIUM	Sr	87.62	ALKALINE

From Strontian, Scotland; discovered 1790; a rare metal which is a sort of evil alter ego of life-supporting calcium. Radioactive strontium 90 is present in atomic fall-out. It is absorbed by bone tissue in place of calcium, and enough of it destroys marrow and can cause cancer.

39　　YTTRIUM　　　Y　　88.9　　EARLY TRANS METALS
From the town of Ytterby, Sweden, where it was discovered in 1794; a scaly metal with an iron-grey sheen. Yttrium 90, a radioactive isotope, has a dramatic medical use in needles which have replaced the surgeon's knife in killing pain-transmitting nerves in the spinal cord.

40　　ZIRCONIUM　　Zr　　91.22　　EARLY TRANS METALS
From zircon, the name of the semiprecious gemstone in which it was discovered in 1789. A metal unaffected by neutrons, zirconium serves as the inner lining of reactors in nuclear submarines and atomic power plants. It is also used as a building material for jets and rockets.

41　　NIOBIUM　　　Nb　　92.906　　EARLY TRANS METALS
From Niobe, daughter of the mythical Greek king Tantalus (niobium is found with tantalum); discovered 1801. Used in steel, atomic reactors, jet engines and rockets, it was known until 1950 as columbium, from Columbus – a poetic name for America, where its ore was first discovered.

42　　MOLYBDENUM　Mo　　95.94　　EARLY TRANS METALS
From molybdos, or lead – first found in what was first thought to be lead-ore; discovered 1778. Fifth highest melting metal, it is used in boiler plate, rifle barrels and filaments. No vessel could be found in which to cast it until a special water-cooled crucible was devised in 1959.

43　　TECHNETIUM　Tc　　(98)　　EARLY TRANS METALS
From technetos, or artificial; produced 1937. The first man-made element, it was originally produced by the atomic bombardment of molybdenum. Later it was found among the fission products of uranium.

44　　RUTHENIUM　　Ru　　101.07　　THE TRIADS
From Ruthenia, Latin for Russia; discovered 1844. Pure ruthenium is too hard and brittle to machine. It makes a top-notch "hardener", however, when it is alloyed with platinum. But used in excess of 15%, ruthenium is ruinous, making the metals too hard to be worked.

Atomic Number	Element	Symbol	Atomic Weight	Family
45	RHODIUM	Rh	102.91	THE TRIADS

From rhodon, or rose (its salts give a rosy solution); discovered 1803. Besides forming alloys, rhodium makes a lustrous, hard coating for other metals in such items as table silver and camera parts. A thin film of vaporized rhodium deposited on glass makes excellent mirrors.

46	PALLADIUM	Pd	106.4	THE TRIADS

After the asteroid Pallas; discovered 1803. Free from tarnish and corrosion-resistant, palladium is incorporated in contacts for telephone relays and high-grade surgical instruments. It is also used with gold, silver and other metals as a "stiffener" in dental inlays and bridgework.

47	SILVER	Ag	107.87	LATE TRANS METALS

From Old English seolfor, for silver; symbol Ag from its Latin name argentum; prehistoric; the best conductor of heat and electricity. Its salts are basic in photography; when silver bromide is exposed to light, it undergoes a chemical change which the developer then makes visible.

48	CADMIUM	Cd	112.4	LATE TRANS METALS

From kadmia, or earth; discovered 1817. Cadmium occurs in nature with zinc. It makes excellent neutron-eating rods to slow up atomic chain reactions and finds use in nickel-cadmium batteries. Its bright sulphide makes the artist's popular pigment, cadmium yellow.

49	INDIUM	In	114.82	BORON/CARBON

From the indigo blue it shows in a spectroscope; discovered 1863. A metal used in engine bearings, in transistors and as a "glue" that adheres to glass, it is too scarce for large-scale use. But a minuscule, long-lived indium battery has been devised to power new electronic wrist watches.

50	TIN	Sn	118.69	BORON/CARBON

An old English word; symbol Sn from stannum, Latin for tin. Prehistoric. Because it does not rust and resists other corrosion, tin has made possible the housewife's delight, canned food. A tin can is steel coated with about 0.0005 of an inch of tin. Over 40,000 million cans are made each year.

51	ANTIMONY	Sb	121.75	NITROGEN/OXYGEN

From antimonas, "opposed to solitude" (it generally occurs mixed with other elements); symbol Sb from stibium, or mark (it was once used as eyebrow pencil). Discovered about 1450. Antimony is mixed with lead in batteries and goes into type metal and pewter alloys.

52 TELLURIUM Te 127.60 NITROGEN/OXYGEN
From tellus, the earth; discovered 1782. With both metallic and non-metallic traits, tellurium has several peculiarities. It is "out of step" in the periodic table, having a lower atomic number but higher atomic weight than iodine. And inhaling its vapour results in garlicky breath.

53 IODINE I 126.90 THE HALOGENS
From iodes, or violet; discovered 1811. A blue-black solid which turns into a violet vapour when heated. Formerly prepared from seaweed, it is now produced from oil-well brines. Most table salt is now "iodized" to supplement the human diet; an iodine deficiency causes thyroid trouble.

54 XENON Xe 131.3 NOBLE GASES
From xenos, or stranger; discovered 1898. The rarest gas in the atmosphere, xenon is used in specialised light sources such as the high-speed electronic flash bulbs used by photographers. In these, the high volatility of its electron structure produces an instant, intense light.

55 CAESIUM Cs 132.91 ALKALINE
From caesius, or sky-blue (its salts turn flames blue); discovered 1860; the softest metal, liquid at warm room temperature, 28°C. Extremely reactive, it finds limited use in vacuum tubes and in atomic clocks so accurate that they vary no more than five seconds in 10 generations.

56 BARIUM Ba 137.3 ALKALINE
From barys, heavy or dense; discovered 1808. The white sulphate is drunk as a medical cocktail to outline the stomach and intestines for X-ray examination. Barium nitrate gives fireworks a green colour.

57 LANTHANUM La 138.91 EARLY TRANS METALS
From lanthanein, to lie hidden; discovered 1839; highly reactive. Because it gives glass special light-bending, or "refractive", properties, lanthanum is used in expensive camera lenses. Radioactive lanthanum has been tested for use in treating cancer.

58 CERIUM Ce 140.12 RARE EARTH METALS
After the asteroid Ceres; discovered 1803; most abundant of the rare-earth elements. It is the chief ingredient (just under 50%) of misch-metal alloy. Cerium is used in alloys to make heat-resistant jet-engine parts; its oxide is a promising new petroleum-cracking catalyst.

142

Atomic		Atomic	
Number	Element	Symbol	Weight	Family

59   PRASEODYMIUM   Pr   140.91   RARE EARTH METALS
From prasios didymos, or green twin (from its green salts); discovered 1885 when separated from its rare-earth twin neodymium. Together they are now used in making lenses for glassmaker's goggles because they filter out the yellow light present in glass blowing.

60   NEODYMIUM   Nd   144.24   RARE EARTH METALS
From neos didymos, or new twin; discovered 1885. In a pure form, it produces the only bright-purple glass known. In a cruder state, it is used to take colour out of glass and to make special glass that transmits the tanning rays of the sun but not the unwanted infrared heat rays.

61   PROMETHIUM   Pm   (145)   RARE EARTH METALS
After Prometheus; discovered 1947; the only rare earth that has never been found in nature. Produced in nuclear reactors, radioactive promethium in an "atomic battery" no bigger than a drawing pin powers guided-missile instruments, watches and radios.

62   SAMARIUM   Sm   150.36   RARE EARTH METALS
From the mineral samarskite, named after a Russian mine official, Colonel V.E. Samarsky; discovered 1879. Calcium chloride crystals treated with samarium have been employed in lasers – devices for producing beams of light intense enough to burn metal or bounce off the moon.

63   EUROPIUM   Eu   151.96   RARE EARTH METALS
From Europe; discovered 1896. Most reactive rare earth. The metal had virtually no practical use until the atomic age. But atom for atom europium can absorb more neutrons than any other element, making it valuable in control rods for nuclear reactors.

64   GADOLINIUM   Gd   157.25   RARE EARTH METALS
From the mineral gadolinite, named after a Finnish chemist; discovered 1880. Falling in the middle of the rare-earth series, gadolinium divides the lighter metals, which tend to impart pliant qualities to alloys, from the heavier metals, used mostly as strengthening agents.

65   TERBIUM   Tb   158.9   RARE EARTH METALS
From Ytterby, Sweden; discovered 1843; named after the town that also gave its name to three other elements; the rare earths ytterbium and erbium and the transition metal yttrium. Like all rare earths, terbium in an impure state is pyrophoric – i.e. it bursts into flame when heated.

143

Atomic Number	Element	Symbol	Atomic Weight	Family

66   DYSPROSIUM   Dy   162.50   RARE EARTH METALS
From dysprositos, or hard to get at; discovered 1886. Dysprosium's chief practical use is in nuclear reactors, where it serves as a nuclear "poison" – i.e. it is employed as a neutron-eating material to keep the neutron-spawning atomic chain reaction from getting out of hand.

67   HOLIUM   Ho   164.93   RARE EARTH METALS
From Holmia, Latin name for Stockholm; discovered 1879. Like dysprosium, holmium is a metal which can absorb fission-bred neutrons. It is used in nuclear reactors as a burnable poison – i.e. one that burns up while it is keeping a chain reaction from running out of control.

68   ERBIUM   Er   167.26   RARE EARTH METALS
From Ytterby, Sweden; discovered 1843. Used in ceramics as erbium oxide to produce a pink glaze. Erbium, holmium and dysprosium are almost identical in terms of their chemical and physical properties. They vary from each other only by one electron in their third inner orbit.

69   THULIUM   Tm   168.93   RARE EARTH METALS
From Thule, or Northland; discovered 1879. When irradiated in a nuclear reactor, thulium produces an isotope that gives off X-rays. A "button" of this isotope is used to make a lightweight, portable X-ray machine for medical use. The "hot" thulium is replaced every few months.

70   YTTERBIUM   Yb   173.04   RARE EARTH METALS
From Ytterby, Sweden; discovered 1907. This element is still little more than a laboratory curiosity. Along with the other rare earths, it recently turned up in the USSR in a mineral called gagarinite after the first astronaut. Easily oxidized.

71   LUTETIUM   Lu   174.97   RARE EARTH METALS
From Lutetia, the ancient name for Paris; discovered 1907; heaviest of the rare earths. Although rare-earth alloys such as misch metal are relatively cheap, pure lutetium is highly expensive. With many of its chemical and physical properties unknown, it has no practical value.

72   HAFNIUM   Hf   178.49   EARLY TRANS METALS
From Hafnia, the Latin name for Copenhagen; discovered 1923. A "wonder metal" of the atomic age, hafnium has a great appetite for neutrons. Thus it goes into neutron-absorbing reactor control rods which slow down nuclear chain reactions and also quench atomic "fires".

144

Atomic Number	Element	Symbol	Atomic Weight	Family

73   TANTALUM   Ta   180.95   EARLY TRANS METALS
From King Tantalus of Greek myth; discovered 1802. Almost impervious to corrosion, tantalum is vital in surgical repairs of the human body; it can replace bone (for example in skull plates); as foil or wire it connects torn nerves; as woven gauze it binds up abdominal muscles.

74   TUNGSTEN   W   183.85   EARLY TRANS METALS
From Swedish tung sten, or heavy stone; symbol W from its German name wolfram; discovered 1783. The highest melting of metals – at 3,410°C – tungsten in filaments withstands intense heat in light bulbs. New tungsten-tipped "painless" dental drills spin at ultra-high speed.

75   RHENIUM   Re   186.2   EARLY TRANS METALS
From the Rhine provinces of Germany; discovered 1925. Rhenium is the ninth scarcest element and has the second highest melting point. It is used in "thermocouples" (electric thermometers for measuring high temperatures) and in the contact points of electrical switches.

76   OSMIUM   Os   190.2   THE TRIADS
From osme, or odour; discovered 1804. A metal with a pungent smell, it is used to produce alloys of extreme hardness. Pen tips and "lifetime" gramophone needles are 60% osmium. It is the densest metal known: a brick-sized chunk of osmium weighs about 56 pounds.

77   IRIDIUM   Ir   192.2   THE TRIADS
From iris, or rainbow, so named for its colourful salts; discovered 1804. Very hard and hence extremely difficult to work or cast, iridium hardens other metals. Its alloys make bars used as standard weights and measures. The international "standard metre" is platinum-iridium.

78   PLATINUM   Pt   195.08   THE TRIADS
From platina, or little silver; discovered 16th century. Found in nuggets of up to 21 pounds, it is used not only in weights and measures but also in catalysts, delicate instruments and electrical equipment. Its cost (more than gold) has demanded a hallmark for platinum jewellery.

79   GOLD   Au   196.97   LATE TRANS METALS
From the old English word geolo, or yellow; symbol Au from its Latin name aurum; prehistoric; the most malleable metal. Man's lust for gold has been a delusion, for he has pursued little more than

a yellow gleam. It cannot be used for much besides money, jewellery and dental work.

| 80 | MERCURY | Hg | 200.59 | LATE TRANS METALS |

From the planet Mercury; symbol Hg from hydrargyrum, or liquid silver; prehistoric. It appears in the glass tubing of thermometers and barometers; it also finds use in "silver" dental inlays and in silent electric switches. Vaporized mercury fills modern blue-hued street lights.

| 81 | THALLIUM | Tl | 204.38 | BORON/CARBON |

From thallos, or a young shoot – its spectrum is a bright-green line; discovered 1861. Its chief use is in thallium sulphate – a deadly rat poison. Odourless and tasteless, it is mixed with starch, sugar, glycerine and water to make an inviting if ominous "treat" for household rodents.

| 82 | LEAD | Pb | 207.2 | BORON/CARBON |

From old English lead; symbol Pb from its Latin name, plumbum, also the origin of plumber. Prehistoric. Enormously durable, lead has been the backbone of plumbing for centuries. Lead pipes once used to drain the baths of ancient Rome have been uncovered still in working order.

| 83 | BISMUTH | Bi | 208.98 | NITROGEN/OXYGEN |

From the German wissmuth, or white mass; discovered 1450. The most metallic member of its family, bismuth melts at 271°C but forms alloys that melt at as low as 47°C. These find wide application in electric fuses, solders and in automatic fire-sprinkler systems.

| 84 | POLONIUM | Po | (209) | NITROGEN/OXYGEN |

After Poland; found in 1898 by Pierre and Marie Curie in pitchblende. The sçarcest natural element, it was the first to be discovered by the Curies. It is sold as an alpha-particle source for scientific use.

| 85 | ASTATINE | At | (210) | THE HALOGENS |

From astatos, or unstable; discovered 1940. Astatine, prepared by bombarding bismuth atoms with helium nuclei, is radioactive and has a maximum half-life of 8.3 hours. Its detection is recorded in the notebook of one of its discoverers, American physicist D. R. Corson.

| 86 | RADON | Rn | (222) | NOBLE GASES |

From radium; discovered 1900. Heaviest gaseous element, it is emitted by radium and is itself radioactive; it decays into radioactive polonium and alpha rays. This radiation makes radon useful in

146

cancer therapy; gold needles filled with the gas are implanted into the diseased tissue.

87   FRANCIUM   Fr   (223)   ALKALINE
From France; discovered 1939. A short-lived product of the decay of actinium, francium has never actually been seen. A graph identifies francium by its radiation in the notebook of its discoverer, Marguerite Perey, a one-time assistant to Marie Curie.

88   RADIUM   Ra   (226)   ALKALINE
From radius, or ray; discovered 1898 by Pierre and Marie Curie; sixth rarest of the elements. Radium bromide mixed with zinc sulphide is a mixture used in luminous watch dials. The radium gives off dangerous radiation which causes the zinc sulphide to glow.

89   ACTINIUM   Ac   (227)   ACTINIDE
From aktinos, or ray; discovered 1899. Second rarest of the elements. Found in pitchblende. With a half-life of 22 years, actinium decomposes into francium and helium.

90   THORIUM   Th   232.04   ACTINIDE
From Thor, Scandinavian war-god; discovered 1828. Thorium can be used instead of scarce uranium as a reactor fuel because it is readily converted into uranium. Almost as abundant as lead, earthly thorium stores more energy than all uranium, coal, oil and other fuels combined.

91   PROTACTINIUM   Pa   (231)   ACTINIDE
From protos, or first; it is the parent of actinium, which is formed by its radioactive decay; discovered 1917. Third rarest of the elements, it can be prepared by modern chemical techniques from thorium or uranium.

92   URANIUM   U   238.03   ACTINIDE
After the planet Uranus; discovered 1789; the heaviest atom among the natural elements. Its most common form has a half-life of 4,500 million years. In a nuclear reactor, it generates neutrons to keep the chain reaction going.

93   NEPTUNIUM   Np   (237)   ACTINIDE
After Neptune, the planet beyond Uranus; discovered 1940. Detected first in invisible, unweighable amounts, neptunium was the first "synthetic" element made from uranium. Traces of it turn up in uranium ores, produced by stray neutrons from uranium's decay.

Atomic Number	Element	Symbol	Atomic Weight	Family

94   PLUTONIUM   Pu   (244)   ACTINIDE

After Pluto, the planet beyond Neptune; discovered 1940. Plutonium was used, instead of uranium, in several of the first atomic bombs. In one of the codes of wartime physicists, plutonium was referred to as "copper"; copper itself had to be renamed "honest-to-God copper".

95   AMERICIUM   Am   (243)   ACTINIDE

Named after the Americas, by analogy with the rare earth europium; discovered 1944. Americium is produced by bombarding plutonium with neutrons. It has been made in gramme quantities which, in the world of such elements, is virtually a superabundance.

96   CURIUM   Cm   (247)   ACTINIDE

In honour of Pierre and Marie Curie, pioneers in the field of radioactivity; discovered 1944. Curium, with a half-life of 19 years, is a decay product of americium. Curium hydroxide is the first known curium compound.

97   BERKELIUM   Bk   (247)   ACTINIDE

After Berkeley, the home of the University of California, whose scientists have detected all 11 of the transuranium elements; discovered 1949. Many inifinitesimal samples of berkelium have been prepared.

98   CALIFORNIUM   Cf   (251)   ACTINIDE

After the State and University of California; discovered 1950. Not until 1960 did californium exist in visible amounts.

99   EINSTEINIUM   Es   (252)   ACTINIDE

After Albert Einstein; discovered 1952. It was first detected in the debris from the 1952 H-bomb explosion at Eniwetok in the Pacific after tons of radioactive coral from atolls in the blast area were sifted and examined. The element was later made in a nuclear reactor.

100   FERMIUM   Fm   (257)   ACTINIDE

After Enrico Fermi; discovered 1953. Fermium, like einsteinium, was first isolated from the debris of the 1952 H-bomb test, having been produced from the fission of uranium. Because of its short life-span, scientists doubt that enough fermium will ever be obtained to be weighed.

101   MENDELEVIUM   Md   (258)   ACTINIDE

After Dmitri Mendeleyev, who devised the periodic table; discovered in 1955. Bombarding the scantest unweighable quantities of einsteinium with helium nuclei, scientists identified mendelevium from the barest shred of evidence – one to three atoms per bombardment.

102   NOBELIUM   No   (259)   ACTINIDE
After Alfred Nobel. A 1957 claim of discovery is disputed, but nobelium was positively identified in 1958 by a team of University of California scientists. Observations were not made on nobelium itself but on atoms of fermium 250 – "daughter atoms" produced by nobelium's decay.

103   LAWRENCIUM   Lr   (260)   ACTINIDE
After Ernest O. Lawrence. Discovered in 1961 at Lawrence Radiation Laboratories, lawrencium was made by bombardment of californium with boron in a chamber fitted with a copper conveyor; the new atoms, one at a time, were carried to a radiation detector for identification.

104   UNNILQUADIUM   Unq   (261)   ACTINIDE
Originally named after Lord Ernest Rutherford, was produced in 1969 at Lawrence Radiation Laboratory by bombardment of californium with carbon nuclei. Soviet scientists had earlier announced the discovery of element 104, but this was not accepted internationally.

105   UNNIPENTIUM   Unp   (262)   ACTINIDE
Originally named after Otto Hahn of Germany, one of the discoverers of uranium fission. It was synthesized in 1970 by bombardment of californium with nitrogen nuclei. The name of this element was recently confirmed by the International Union of Pure and Applied Chemistry.

CHAPTER THIRTEEN

RED WINES OF BORDEAUX

Region	Chateaux	Vintage	Growth	Mature	Rating
St.-Estephe Description: Blackcurrant fruit, massive	Cos D'Estournel	1982	2nd	1995–2020	97
St.-Estephe Fruity, tannic, big	Cos D'Estournel	1961	2nd	1986–2000	91
Pauillac Fruity lushness, big	Latour	1982	1st	1995–2025	97
Pauillac Velvety, spicy oak	Latour	1981	1st	1991–2005	90
Pauillac Stunningly big bouquet, black-currant fruit	Latour	1978	1st	1992–2010	95
Pauillac Whiff of cedar and walnuts	Latour	1975	1st	2000–2030	93
Pauillac Very concentrated and dense	Latour	1970	1st	2000–2030	96
Pauillac Bouquet of leather, spices and tobacco	Latour	1966	1st	1988–2005	95
Pauillac Rich, round, supple	Latour	1964	1st	Now–1997	92
Pauillac Concentrated, rich flavours	Latour	1962	1st	1985–1995	91

Region	Chateaux	Vintage	Growth	Mature	Rating
Pauillac Syrupy, port-like, phenomenal bouquet	**Latour**	1961	1st	2000–2050	100
Pauillac Opulence, concentration	**Mouton-Rothschild**	1982	1st	1995–2025	100
Pauillac Dusty, leathery texture, chewy	**Mouton-Rothschild**	1975	1st	1995–2020	90
Pauillac Herbaceous aromas, powerful	**Mouton-Rothschild**	1970	1st	1995–2030	95
Pauillac Tightly restrained flavour, evolving bouquet	**Mouton-Rothschild**	1966	1st	1990–2010	92
Pauillac Olfactory, silky	**Mouton-Rothschild**	1962	1st	Now/ drink up!	90
Pauillac Fat on palate, multi-scented bouquet	**Mouton–Rothschild**	1961	1st	1992–2020	96
Pauillac Tough, fleshy texture, impressive	**Lafite-Rothschild**	1983	1st	2005–2035	92
Pauillac Huge bouquet, concentrated	**Lafite-Rothschild**	1982	1st	2000–2030	96
Pauillac Promising, full-bodied	**Lafite-Rothschild**	1981	1st	2000–2025	93
Pauillac Tight but complex bouquet, medium body	**Lafite-Rothschild**	1979	1st	1988–2005	90
Pauillac Ripe, savoury and fruity	**Lafite-Rothschild**	1978	1st	1988–2005	90

Region	Chateaux	Vintage	Growth	Mature	Rating
Pauillac Stunning, beautiful seductive bouquet	**Lafite-Rothschild**	1976	1st	1990–2010	96
Pauillac Cedary, fruity, explodes, full body	**Lafite-Rothschild**	1975	1st	1990–2010	96
Pauillac Intense bouquet, violet-scented fruit, full bodied	**Pichon-Longueville**	1983	2nd	1995–2015	94
Pauillac Intensely fruity, viscous wine	**Pichon-Longueville**	1982	2nd	1992–2010	94
Pauillac Supple, fat, silky	**Pichon-Longueville**	1981	2nd	1988–1998	91
Pauillac Velvety, rich and gentle	**Pichon-Longueville**	1979	2nd	1987–1998	93
Pauillac Deepest, richest and lush	**Pichon-Longueville**	1978	2nd	1988–2005	94
Pauillac Ripe, plummy fruit and fresh robustness	**Pichon-Longueville**	1975	2nd	1990–2010	92
Pauillac Big, rich, bouquet exotic	**Pichon-Longueville**	1970	2nd	1986–2000	91
Pauillac Dark, plummy bouquet, viscous	**Pichon-Longueville**	1961	2nd	Now–2003	95
St.-Julien Voluptuous, stunning density	**Ducru-Beaucaillou**	1982	2nd	1994–2015	96

Region	Chateaux	Vintage	Growth	Mature	Rating
St.-Julien Deft, touch of oak, ageing, beautifully crafted wine	**Ducru-Beaucaillou**	1981	2nd	1993–2008	90
St.-Julien Deep, savoury flavours and multi-dimensional bouquet	**Ducru-Beaucaillou**	1978	2nd	1990–2015	90
St.-Julien Ripe fruit and spicy oak, charm and appeal	**Ducru-Beaucaillou**	1970	2nd	1986–2000	91
St.-Julien Exotic bouquet, rich, caressing the palate	**Ducru-Beaucaillou**	1961	2nd	Now–1992	93
St.-Julien An infant giant, explosively fruity	**Leoville-Las Cases**	1983	2nd	1998–2020	90
St.-Julien Monumental, intense and tannic	**Leoville-Las Cases**	1982	2nd	2000–2030	97
St.-Julien Immense potential, full deep flavours, stunning	**Leoville-Las Cases**	1978	2nd	1994–2015	92
St.-Julien Deep, ripe bouquet, aggressively tannic	**Leoville-Las Cases**	1975	2nd	1995–2030	92
St.-Julien Perfectly balanced and excellent fruity intensity	**Leoville-Las Cases**	1966	2nd	1966–1997	90
St.-Julien Plummy, extract of fruit	**Gruaud-Larose**	1983	2nd	1995–2015	90

Region	Chateaux	Vintage	Growth	Mature	Rating
St.-Julien Incredibly rich, deliciously viscous, extremely tannic	**Gruaud-Larose**	1982	2nd	1995–2015	96
St.-Julien Mouth puckering tannins, promising bouquet	**Gruaud-Larose**	1975	2nd	1995–2025	90
St.-Julien Powerful, fresh, densely concentrated	**Gruaud-Larose**	1961	2nd	1987–2020	95
Margaux/ S. Medoc Astonishingly rich, concentrated, deep flavours	**Margaux**	1983	1st	1998–2030	96
Margaux/ S. Medoc Celestial wine, richly textured fruit and significant tannins	**Margaux**	1982	1st	1995–2025	96
Margaux/ S. Medoc Precocious and less weighty, concentrated tannic	**Margaux**	1981	1st	1991–2010	92
Margaux/ S. Medoc Tell-tale haunting, violet aroma	**Margaux**	1979	1st	1990–2005	93
Margaux/ S. Medoc Harmony and seductive bouquet	**Margaux**	1978	1st	1990–2015	94

Region	Chateaux	Vintage	Growth	Mature	Rating
Margaux/ S. Medoc Top flight, intense bouquet	**Margaux**	1961	1st	1987–1992	92
Margaux/ S. Medoc Full intensity, plummy, chewy, powerful	**Palmer**	1983	3rd	1995–2010	90
Margaux/ S. Medoc Superstar, peppery, velvety	**Palmer**	1978	3rd	1989–2005	91
Margaux/ S. Medoc Uncommonly powerful, loaded with fruit and tannin	**Palmer**	1975	3rd	1990–2020	92
Margaux/ S. Medoc Intense, berryish aroma, full-bodied	**Palmer**	1970	3rd	1988–2005	94
Margaux/ S. Medoc Sensational bouquet, velvety richness	**Palmer**	1966	3rd	1986–2000	96
Margaux/ S. Medoc Perfumed, opulent, multi-dimensional	**Palmer**	1961	3rd	1987–1992	96
Graves Monumental huge, spicy	**La Mission-Haut-Brion**	1982	Cru Classé	1994–2015	95
Graves Prominent vanillin, cassis fruit	**La Mission-Haut-Brion**	1981	Cru Classé	1991–2000	90

Region	Chateaux	Vintage	Growth	Mature	Rating
Graves Gravelly, scented bouquet, fruity flavours	**La Mission-Haut-Brion**	1978	Cru Classé	1990–2010	94
Graves Monumental magnificent iron-like mineral scents and smoky oak	**La Mission-Haut-Brion**	1975	Cru Classé	1990–2025	100
Graves Deep, spicy and full	**La Mission-Haut-Brion**	1970	Cru Classé	1990–2005	92
Graves Complex, cedary, tobacco-scented aroma	**La Mission-Haut-Brion**	1966	Cru Classé	1986–1995	91
Graves Enormous concentration of fruit, full intensity	**La Mission-Haut-Brion**	1964	Cru Classé	1987–1997	93
Graves Fabulous bouquet, full-bodied	**La Mission-Haut-Brion**	1961	Cru Classé	1987–2010	96
Graves Gorgeous bouquet, vanillin oakiness, unctuous with layers of fruit	**Haut-Brion**	1982	1st	1995–2015	96
Graves Complex bouquet, earthy scents, balance, power, harmony	**Haut-Brion**	1979	1st	1992–2005	90
Graves Seductively rich, supple, round and generous	**Haut-Brion**	1978	1st	1990–2000	90

Region	Chateaux	Vintage	Growth	Mature	Rating
Graves Splendidly rich, mineral scented, voluptuous flavours	**Haut-Brion**	1964	1st	1987–1995	90
Graves Intensity of fruit, chewy texture, spicy bouquet	**Haut-Brion**	1961	1st	1987–1992	93
Graves Massive, exceptional length, tannic	**La Tour-Haut-Brion**	1982	Cru Classé	1996–2015	94
Graves Bouquet of great penetration, explodes, full-bodied	**La Tour-Haut-Brion**	1975	Cru Classé	1995–2020	96
Graves Chewy, opulent, massively proportioned	**La Tour-Haut-Brion**	1961	Cru Classé	1990–2030	95
Pomerol Voluptuous, decadently concentrated fruit	**Petrus**	1982	Unclas.	1995–2030	100
Pomerol Bouquet explodes, grilled almonds and toffee, multi-dimensional	**Petrus**	1981	Unclas.	1997–2025	95
Pomerol Large framed, tannic, dense	**Petrus**	1979	Unclas.	1993–2015	92
Pomerol Blockbuster, opulent, massive	**Petrus**	1975	Unclas.	2000–2050	98

Region	Chateaux	Vintage	Growth	Mature	Rating
Pomerol Velvety, silky ripe fruit	**Petrus**	1971	Unclas.	1987–2000	95
Pomerol Jammy, full-bodied	**Petrus**	1970	Unclas.	1990–2020	93
Pomerol Chunky, fleshy, warm and generous	**Petrus**	1967	Unclas.	1987–1994	90
Pomerol Intense aromas, powerful, multi-dimensional	**Petrus**	1964	Unclas.	1987–1997	97
Pomerol Warm melted buttery caramel and toasty vanillin oak	**Petrus**	1961	Unclas.	1987–2003	100
Pomerol Avalanche of rich, ripe fruit, hint of fresh leather	**Trotanoy**	1982	Unclas.	1997–2020	96
Pomerol Fleshy, full body and bouquet	**Trotanoy**	1975	Unclas.	1988–2010	93
Pomerol Velvety, ripe, decadent, young	**Trotanoy**	1971	Unclas.	1985–1992	92
Pomerol Proportioned, broodingly dark	**Trotanoy**	1970	Unclas.	1990–2006	90
Pomerol Massively rich, unctuous texture, sweet	**Trotanoy**	1961	Unclas.	1987–2007	95
Pomerol Unbelievable bouquet, full-bodied, viscous	**Lafleur**	1975	Unclas.	1990–2015	96

Region	Chateaux	Vintage	Growth	Mature	Rating
Pomerol Succulent, staggering concentration, sensational bouquet	**Latour a Pomerol**	1961	Unclas.	1987–1997	98
Pomerol Explosive, jammy, intense, voluptuous	**L'Evangile**	1982	Unclas.	1992–2005	96
St.-Emilion Big-boned, deeply concentrated	**Cheval Blanc**	1983	Prem. Grand Cru Classé	1995–2020	93
St.-Emilion Exotic aroma, intense fruit interplay, opulent	**Cheval Blanc**	1982	Prem. Grand Cru Classé	1992–2015	98
St.-Emilion Relatively rich, plummy, silky, layered flavours	**Cheval Blanc**	1981	Prem. Grand Cru Classé	1989–2000	90
St.-Emilion The best weight and richness, bouquet, full bodied	**Cheval Blanc**	1975	Prem. Grand Cru Classé	1990–2020	92
St.-Emilion Powerful yet restrained, new wood and gravelly	**Cheval Blanc**	1964	Prem. Grand Cru Classé	1985–2000	95
St.-Emilion Earthy, gravelly and full blown bouquet	**Cheval Blanc**	1961	Prem. Grand Cru Classé	1987–?	94
St.-Emilion Full-bodied, jammy and rich	**Ausone**	1983	Prem. Grand Cru Classé	1992–2005	90

Region	Chateaux	Vintage	Growth	Mature	Rating
St.-Emilion Concentrated, full-bodied, backward	**Ausone**	1982	Prem. Grand Cru Classé	2000–2040	94
St.-Emilion Voluptuous, intense, complex bouquet	**Ausone**	1976	Prem. Grand Cru Classé	1988–2000	90

CHAPTER FOURTEEN

SOLAR SYSTEM

The 43 Major Members of Our Solar System

Celestial Body/Satellite	*Diameter*	*Orbit Diameter (mi.)*
Sun The sun rotates on its axis once each 25.38 days. It is a medium-sized star, of a colour type called yellow.	864,950	–
Mercury Mercury rotates on its axis once each 58.5 days and orbits the sun once each 87.9 days. Its maximum surface temperature is a blazing 770°F.	3,000	36,000,000
Venus Venus rotates on its axis once each 243 days and orbits the sun once each 224.7 days. Under the planet's thick cloud cover of carbon dioxide and nitrogen, heat accumulates to produce temperatures over 750°F.	7,700	67,200,000
Earth Life thrives on this planet because it has water, and the earth is just the right distance from the sun so that water can exist here as a liquid. Temperatures: −126.9°–136.4°F.	7,927	93,000,000
Moon Earth, for its size, has the largest satellite of any planet in the solar system.	2,158	238,840
Mars Mars' day is 24.6 hours long. It is the most likely of all the planets to have life on it, with a sparse atmosphere of carbon dioxide and traces of water. The	4,219	141,600,000

Celestial Body/Satellite	Diameter	Orbit Diameter (mi.)
maximum temperature on Mars is 80°F on the equator at noon. Average temperature is −60°F. Lows range below −100°F.		
Deimos Smallest known satellite in the solar system.	5	14,600
Phobos	8	5,800
Asteroids The asteroids are huge chunks of rock orbiting the sun between Mars and Jupiter. They are minor planets. There may be as many as 40,000 of them.	1–429	300,000,000 av.
Jupiter Jupiter's atmosphere is largely hydrogen and helium. It is believed that Jupiter would have become a companion star to the sun had it been a little larger.	88,700	484,300,000
Amalthea	150	113,000
Io	2,310	262,000
Europa	1,950	417,000
Ganymede This satellite is larger than the planet Mercury.	3,120	666,000
Callisto	2,770	1,170,000
Hestia	100	7,120,000
Hera	35	7,290,000
Demeter	15	7,300,000
Adrastea	14	13,000,000
Pan	19	14,000,000
Poseidon	35	14,600,000
Hades	17	14,700,000
Saturn Known since ancient times, Saturn is one of two planets with rings. After Galileo introduced the telescope, many theories were proposed about the form	75,100	886,000,000

Celestial Body/Satellite	Diameter	Orbit Diameter (mi.)

of Saturn. It was finally described correctly by Christian Huygens in 1659.

Celestial Body/Satellite	Diameter	Orbit Diameter (mi.)
Janus	190	98,000
Mimas	300	115,000
Enceladus	350	148,000
Tethys	600	183,000
Dione	600	234,000
Rhea	800	327,000
Titan	3,000	758,000

A peculiar combination of circumstances gives Titan a fighting chance for supporting life. Its atmosphere traps and holds what little warmth reaches it at nearly a billion miles from the sun. The greenhouse effect might allow Titan to achieve temperatures similar to those on Mars, within the range suitable for life. The answer may come when an unmanned space vehicle takes a closer look.

Celestial Body/Satellite	Diameter	Orbit Diameter (mi.)
Hyperion	300	919,000
Iapetus	1,000	2,210,000
Phoebe	130	8,040,000
Uranus	29,300	1,780,000,000

The second planet with rings. It's cold on Uranus: alltime high is −310°F. Uranus, the first "discovered" planet, found by accident in 1781 by William Herschel, then an amateur astronomer. When the German chemist Martin Klaproth discovered a new metallic element in 1789, he named it for the new planet: uranium.

Celestial Body/Satellite	Diameter	Orbit Diameter (mi.)
Miranda	190	76,000
Ariel	500	119,000
Umbriel	370	166,000
Titania	680	272,000
Oberon	620	364,000
Neptune	31,200	2,790,000,000

Celestial Body/Satellite	Diameter	Orbit Diameter (mi.)

Neptune was the first planet whose existence was predicted theoretically before it was discovered. Urbain Leverrier, a French astronomer, completed his calculations in 1846, and the planet was discovered within the year.

Celestial Body/Satellite	Diameter	Orbit Diameter (mi.)
Triton	2,300	220,000
Nereid	190	3,500,000
Pluto	3,700	3,670,000,000

Pluto was discovered in March 1930 by Clyde Tombaugh, a U.S. astronomer. The calculations used to predict Pluto's position had been done by another American, Percival Lowell.

CHAPTER FIFTEEN

MEMORISING YOUR LIFE

If you wish to remember the major elements of your past, present and future life, the SEMMG allows you to do so with ease.

Allow one key memory word for each month. In so doing, it is possible for you, by adding a few major items for the month on a Link System, to remember eight years within 100 key image words in the Self-Enhancing Master Memory Grid.

Thus an entire life can be memorised with a thousand!

The following story by Jorge Luis Borges talks of such a life.

Critics are still trying to determine whether the story was a fabrication, or a true reportage.

In view of what you have read so far, and what you will read when you read *Funes, the Memorious*, decide for yourself: was it true? Is it possible?

FUNES, THE MEMORIOUS

I remember him (I scarcely have the right to use this ghostly verb; only one man on earth deserved the right, and he is dead), I remember him with a dark passionflower in his hand, looking at it as no one has ever looked at such a flower, though they might look from the twilight of day until the twilight of night, for a whole life long. I remember him, his face immobile and Indian-like, and singularly *remote*, behind his cigarette. I remember (I believe) the strong delicate fingers of the plainsman who can braid leather. I remember, near those hands, a vessel in which to make maté tea, bearing the arms of the Banda Oriental;* I remember, in the window of the house,

*The Eastern Shore (of the Uruguay River); now the Orient Republic of Uruguay. – *Editor's note.*

a yellow rush mat, and beyond, a vague marshy landscape. I remember clearly his voice, the deliberate, resentful nasal voice of the old Eastern Shore man, without the Italianate syllables of today, I did not see him more than three times; the last time, in 1887 . . .

That all those who knew him should write something about him seems to me a very felicitous idea; my testimony may perhaps be the briefest and without doubt the poorest, and it will not be the least impartial. The deplorable fact of my being an Argentinian will hinder me from falling into a dithyramb – an obligatory form in the Uruguay, when the theme is an Uruguayan.

Littérateur, slicker, Buenos Airean: Funes did not use these insulting phrases, but I am sufficiently aware that for him I represented these unfortunate categories. Pedro Leandro Ipuche has written that Funes was a precursor of the superman, 'an untamed and vernacular Zarathustra'; I do not doubt it, but one must not forget, either, that he was a countryman from the town of Fray Bentos, with certain incurable limitations.

My first recollection of Funes is quite clear, I see him at dusk, sometimes in March or February of the year '84. That year, my father had taken me to spend the summer at Fray Bentos. I was on my way back from the farm at San Francisco with my cousin Bernardo Haedo. We came back singing, on horseback; and this last fact was not the only reason for my joy. After a sultry day, an enormous slate-grey storm had obscured the sky. It was driven on by a wind from the south; the trees were already tossing like madmen; and I had the apprehension (the secret hope) that the elemental downpour would catch us out in the open. We were running a kind of race with the tempest. We rode into a narrow lane which wound down between two enormously high brick footpaths. It had grown black of a sudden; I now heard rapid almost secret steps above; I raised my eyes and saw a boy running along the narrow, cracked path as if he were running along a narrow, broken wall. I remember the loose trousers, tight at the bottom, the hemp sandals; I remember the cigarette in the hard visage, standing out against the by now limitless darkness. Bernardo unexpectedly yelled to him: 'What's the time, Ireneo?' Without looking up, without stopping, Ireneo replied: 'In ten minutes it will be eight o'clock, child Bernardo Juan Francisco'. The voice was sharp, mocking.

I am so absentminded that the dialogue which I have just cited would not have penetrated my attention if it had not been repeated by my cousin, who was stimulated, I think, by a certain local pride and by a desire to show himself indifferent to the other's three-sided reply.

He told me that the boy above us in the pass was a certain Ireneo Funes, renowned for a number of eccentricities, such as that of having nothing to do with people and of always knowing the time, like a watch. He added that Ireneo was the son of María Clementina Funes, an ironing woman in the town, and that his father, some people said, was an 'Englishman' named O'Connor, a doctor in the salting fields, though some said the father was a horse-breaker, or scout, from the province of El Salto. Ireneo lived with his mother, at the edge of the country house of the Laurels.

In the years '85 and '86 we spent the summer in the city of Montevideo. We returned to Fray Bentos in '87. As was natural, I inquired after all my acquaintances, and finally, about 'the chronometer Funes'. I was told that he had been thrown by a wild horse at the San Francisco ranch, and that he had been hopelessly crippled. I remember the impression of uneasy magic which the news provoked in me: the only time I had seen him we were on horseback, coming from San Francisco, and he was in a high place; from the lips of my cousin Bernardo the affair sounded like a dream elaborated with elements out of the past. They told me that Ireneo did not move now from his cot, but remained with his eyes fixed on the backyard fig tree, or on a cobweb. At sunset he allowed himself to be brought to the window. He carried pride to the extreme of pretending that the blow which had befallen him was a good thing . . . Twice I saw him behind the iron grate which sternly delineated his eternal imprisonment: unmoving, once, his eyes closed; unmoving also, another time, absorbed in the contemplation of a sweet-smelling sprig of lavender cotton.

At the time I had begun, not without some ostentation, the methodical study of Latin. My valise contained the *De viris*

167

illustribus of Lhomond, the *Thesaurus* of Quicherat, *Caesar's Commentaries,* and an odd-numbered volume of the *Historia Naturalis* of Pliny, which exceeded (and still exceeds) my modest talents as a Latinist. Everything is noised around in a small town; Ireneo, at his small farm on the outskirts,, was not long in learning of the arrival of these anomalous books. He sent me a flowery, ceremonious letter, in which he recalled our encounter, unfortunately brief, 'on the seventh day of February of the year '84,' and alluded to the glorious services which Don Gregorio Haedo, my uncle, dead the same year, 'had rendered to the Two Fatherlands in the glorious campaign of Ituzaingó,' and he solicited the loan of any one of the volumes, to be accompanied by a dictionary 'for the better intelligence of the original text, for I do not know Latin as yet.' He promised to return them in good condition, almost immediately. The letter was perfect, very nicely constructed; the orthography was of the type sponsored by Andrés Bello: *i* for *y, j* for *g.* At first I naturally suspected a jest. My cousins assured me it was not so, that these were the ways of Ireneo. I did not know whether to attribute to impudence, ignorance, or stupidity, the idea that the difficult Latin required no other instrument than a dictionary; in order fully to undeceive him I sent the *Gradus ad Parnassum* of Quicherat, and the Pliny.

On 14 February, I received a telegram from Buenos Aires telling me to return immediately, for my father was 'in no way well.' God forgive me, but the prestige of being the recipient of an urgent telegram, the desire to point out to all of Fray Bentos the contradiction between the negative form of the news and the positive adverb, the temptation to dramatize my sorrow as I feigned a virile stoicism, all no doubt distracted me from the possibility of anguish. As I packed my valise, I noticed that I was missing the *Gradus* and the volume of the *Historia Naturalis.* The 'Saturn' was to weigh anchor on the morning of the next day; that night, after supper, I made my way to the house of Funes. Outside, I was surprised to find the night no less oppressive than the day.

Ireneo's mother received me at the modest ranch.

She told me that Ireneo was in the back room and that I should not be disturbed to find him in the dark, for he knew how to pass the dead hours without lighting the candle. I

crossed the cobblestone patio, the small corridor; I came to the
second patio. A great vine covered everything, so that the
darkness seemed complete. Of a sudden I heard the high-
pitched, mocking voice of Ireneo. The voice spoke in Latin;
the voice (which came out of the obscurity) was reading, with
obvious delight, a treatise or prayer or incantation. The
Roman syllables resounded in the earthen patio; my suspicion
made them seem undecipherable, interminable; afterwards, in
the enormous dialogue of that night, I learned that they made
up the first paragraph of the twenty-fourth chapter of the
seventh book of the *Historia Naturalis*. The subject of this
chapter is memory; the last words are *ut nihil non iisdem verbis
redderetur auditum*.

Without the least change in his voice, Ireneo bade me come
in. He was lying on the cot, smoking. It seems to me that I did
not see his face until dawn; I seem to recall the momentary
glow of the cigarette. The room smelled vaguely of dampness.
I sat down, and repeated the story of the telegram and my
father's illness.

I come now to the most difficult point in my narrative. For
the entire story has no other point (the reader might as well
know it by now) than this dialogue of almost a half-century
ago. I shall not attempt to reproduce his words, now
irrecoverable. I prefer truthfully to make a résumé of the
many things Ireneo told me. The indirect style is remote and
weak; I know that I sacrifice the effectiveness of my narrative;
but let my readers imagine the nebulous sentences which
clouded that night.

Ireneo began by enumerating, in Latin and Spanish, the
cases of prodigious memory cited in the *Historia Naturalis*:
Cyrus, king of the Persians, who could call every soldier in his
armies by name; Mithridates Eupator, who administered
justice in the twenty-two languages of his empire; Simonides,
inventor of mnemotechny; Metrodorus, who practised the art
of repeating faithfully what he heard once. With evident good
faith Funes marvelled that such things should be considered
marvellous. He told me that previous to the rainy afternoon
when the blue-tinted horse threw him, he had been – like any
Christian – blind, deaf-mute, somnambulistic, memoryless. (I
tried to remind him of his precise perception of time, his

memory for proper names; he paid no attention to me). For nineteen years, he said, he had lived like a person in a dream: he looked without seeing, heard without hearing, forgot everything – almost everything. On falling from the horse, he lost consciousness; when he recovered it, the present was almost intolerable it was so rich and bright; the same was true of the most ancient and most trivial memories. A little later he realized that he was crippled. This fact scarcely interested him. He reasoned (or felt) that immobility was a minimum price to pay. And now, his perception and his memory were infallible.

We, in a glance, perceive three wine glasses on the table; Funes saw all the shoots, clusters, and grapes of the vine. He remembered the shapes of the clouds in the south at dawn on the 30th of April of 1882, and he could compare them in his recollection with the marbled grain in the design of a leather-bound book which he had seen only once, and with the lines in the spray which an oar raised in the Rio Negro on the eve of the battle of the Quebracho. These recollections were not simple; each visual image was linked to muscular sensations, thermal sensations, etc. He could reconstruct all his dreams all his fancies. Two or three times he had reconstructed an entire day. He told me: *I have more memories in myself alone than all men have had since the world was a world.* And again: *My dreams are like your vigils.* And again, toward dawn: *My memory, sir, is like a garbage disposal.*

A circumference on a blackboard, a rectangular triangle, a rhomb, are forms which we can fully intuit; the same held true with Ireneo for the tempestuous mane of a stallion, a herd of cattle in a pass, the ever-changing flame or the innumerable ash, the many faces of a dead man during the course of a protracted wake. He could perceive I do not know how many stars in the sky.

These things he told me; neither then nor at any time later did they seem doubtful. In those days neither the cinema nor the phonograph yet existed; nevertheless, it seems strange, almost incredible, that no one should have experimented on Funes. The truth is that we all live by leaving behind; no doubt we all profoundly know that we are immortal and that sooner or later every man will do all things and know everything.

The voice of Funes, out of the darkness, continued. He told me that toward 1886 he had devised a new system of enumeration and that in a very few days he had gone beyond twenty-four thousand. He had not written it down, for what he once meditated would not be erased. The first stimulus to his work, I believe, had been his discontent with the fact that 'thirty-three Uruguayans' required two symbols and three words, rather than a single word and a single symbol. Later he applied his extravagant principle to the other numbers. In place of seven thousand thirteen, he would say (for example) *Máximo Perez*; in place of seven thousand fourteen, *The Train*; other numbers were *Luis Melián Lafinur, Olimar, Brimstone, Clubs, The Whale, Gas, The Cauldron, Napoleon, Agustín de Vedia*. In lieu of five hundred, he would say *nine*. Each word had a particular sign, a species of mark; the last were very complicated. . . . I attempted to explain that this rhapsody of unconnected terms was precisely the contrary of a system of enumeration. I said that to say three hundred and sixty-five was to say three hundreds, six tens, five units: an analysis which does not exist in such numbers as *The Negro Timoteo* or *The Flesh Blanket*. Funes did not understand me, or did not wish to understand me.

Locke, in the seventeenth century, postulated (and re-jected) an impossible idiom in which each individual object, each stone, each bird and branch had an individual name; Fumes had once projected an analogous idiom, but he had renounced it as being too general, too ambiguous. In effect, Funes not only remembered every leaf on every tree of every wood, but even every one of the times he had perceived or imagined it. He determined to reduce all of his past experience to some seventy thousand recollections, which he would later define numerically. Two considerations dissuaded him: the thought that the task was interminable and the thought that it was useless. He knew that at the hour of his death he would scarcely have finished classifying even all the memories of his childhood.

The two projects I have indicated (an infinite vocabulary for the natural series of numbers, and a usable mental catalogue of all the images of memory) are lacking in sense, but they reveal a certain stammering greatness. They allow us to make out dimly, or to infer, the dizzying world of Funes. He was, let us not forget, almost incapable of general, platonic ideas. It was not only difficult for him to understand that the generic term *dog* embraced so many unlike specimens of differing sizes and different forms; he was disturbed by the fact that a dog at three-fourteen (seen in profile) should have the same name as the dog at three-fifteen (seen from the front). His own face in the mirror, his own hands, surprised him on every occasion. Swift writes that the emperor of Lilliput could discern the movement of the minute hand; Funes could continuously make out the tranquil advances of corruption, of caries, of fatigue. He noted the progress of death, of moisture. He was the solitary and lucid spectator of a multiform world which was instantaneously and almost intolerably exact. Babylon, London, and New York have overawed the imagination of men with their ferocious splendour; no one, in those populous towers or upon those surging avenues, has felt the heat and pressure of a reality as indefatigable as that which day and night converged upon the unfortunate Ireneo in his humble South American farmhouse. It was very difficult for him to sleep. To sleep is to be abstracted from the world; Funes, on his back in his cot, in the shadows, imagined every crevice and every moulding of the various houses which surrounded him. (I repeat, the least important of his recollections was more minutely precise and more lively than our perception of a physical pleasure or a physical torment.) Toward the east, in a section which was not yet cut into blocks of homes, there were some new unknown houses. Funes imagined them black, compact, made of a single obscurity; he would turn his face in this direction in order to sleep. He would also imagine himself at the bottom of the river, being rocked and annihilated by the current.

Without effort, he had learned English, French, Portuguese, Latin. I suspect, nevertheless, that he was not very capable of thought. To think is to forget a difference, to generalize, to abstract. In the overly replete world of Funes there were nothing but details, almost contiguous details.

The equivocal clarity of dawn penetrated along the earthen patio.

Then it was that I saw the face of the voice which had

spoken all through the night. Ireneo was nineteen years old; he had been born in 1868; he seemed as monumental as bronze, more ancient than Egypt, anterior to the prophecies and the pyramids. It occurred to me that each one of my words (each one of my gestures) would live on in his implacable memory; I was benumbed by the fear of multiplying super-fluous gestures.

Ireneo Funes died in 1889, of a pulmonary congestion.

1942   *Translated by* ANTHONY KERRIGAN

APPENDIX

J O I N
THE BRAIN CLUB

Meet regularly with others who also wish to expand their MEMORY based on the priciples outlined in *MASTER YOUR MEMORY*.

Increase your reading skills, using the methods described in *SPEED READING*, and competing with others increase your knowledge and mental skills using both books to aid your study techniques.

Each area within *THE BRAIN CLUB* will be graded, and certificates awarded as you reach different levels of competence.

For details of the nearest Cell of THE BRAIN CLUB contact:

> Tony Buzan
> The Harleyford Manor Estate
> Marlow
> Buckinghamshire
> SL7 2DY
> England

The Universal Organiser

This NEW and UNIQUE approach to time and self management is a diary system, based on the techniques taught by Tony Buzan.

The *Universal Organiser* is a living system that GROWS with you, and that provides a comprehensive perspective on your life, your desires, and your business and family functions.

The *Universal Organiser* is the first diary system to use the principles that Leonardo da Vinci discovered in the Italian Renaissance: that images and colour enhance both CREATIVITY and MEMORY, as well as being both more ENJOYABLE and EASY.

The *Universal Organiser* REFLECTS YOU, and gives you the FREEDOM to perform at your Highest Potential.

The *Universal Organiser* is made of materials that are only of the HIGHEST QUALITY, using the best leathers and paper available.

The *Universal Organiser* is designed to help you manage the four main areas of life: HEALTH (mental, physical and emotional); WEALTH; HAPPINESS; and CREATIVITY.

The *Universal Organiser*, in so doing, allows you to ORGANISE your past, present and future in a manner that is both ENJOYABLE and FUN.

The *Universal Organiser's* pages and partitions have been designed to enable you to get a comprehensive perspective on your YEARLY PLAN, your MONTHLY and WEEKLY PLANS, and your DAILY PLAN, using the NEW TWENTY-FOUR HOUR CLOCK, MIND MAPPING, *MASTER YOUR MEMORY* and *SPEED READING* systems.

The *Universal Organiser* is SOLID and EFFICIENT, and reflects the principles outlined in *SPEED READING* and *MASTER YOUR MEMORY*.

For further details contact:

Tony Buzan
The Harleyford Manor Estate
Marlow
Buckinghamshire
SL7 2DY
England

To Improve your Brain Skills Further the Following Aids are Available from:

Tony Buzan
(address as above)

Video Tapes
Use your Head – the original BBC TV series attractively presented with updated Facilitator's Manual and two textbooks.
The Enchanted Loom – Thames Television's one-hour documentary on the brain, featuring interviews with the world's major contributors to the field; devised, and presented by Tony Buzan
Audio Tapes
Learning and Memory – Tony Buzan's record breaking cassette produced for *Psychology Today*.
THE INTELLIGENCE REVOLUTION audio cassette sets:
I. Discussions by the world's leading experts on the brain: Tony Buzan discussing new methods of using MEMORY and general BRAIN SKILLS; Dr. Luis Machado (the world's first

MINISTER FOR INTELLIGENCE, appointed to the Venezuelan Government) discussing the fact that your intelligence CAN be raised; and Dee Dickinson outlining some of the latest research in major brain skill areas.

II. Tony Buzan speaking on the following subjects: LEFT AND RIGHT BRAIN, MEMORY, and MIND MAPPING SKILLS.

The Master Mind Map

A limited edition poster, each numbered copy signed by the artist, depicting in a surrealist manner all the principles taught and explained in the books *SPEED READING* and *MASTER YOUR MEMORY*. This beautiful picture is called 'Body and Soul', and the Swedish artist is Ulf Ekberg.

Further Reading

Use Your Head
Use Your Memory
Speed Reading
Make the Most of Your Mind
The Brain User's Guide
Spore One (Poetry)

Courses

Tony Buzan offers courses for Governments, corporations and educational institutions in:

Memory
Speed Reading
Study Skills
Mind Mapping
Brain Skills
Family Study
Creativity
Use Your Head
Communication Skills
Advanced Memory Skills
Advanced Speed Reading Skills
Advanced Study Techniques

For details contact: Tony Buzan
(address on opposite page)